Turning Knowledge Into Action: What's Data Got to Do With It?

Lisa Petrides

League for Innovation in the Community College

The League for Innovation in the Community College is an international organization dedicated to catalyzing the community college movement. The League hosts conferences and institutes, develops web resources, conducts research, produces publications, provides services, and leads projects and initiatives with more than 750 member colleges, 100 corporate partners, and a host of other government and nonprofit agencies in a continuing effort to make a positive difference for students and communities. Information about the League and its activities is available at www.league.org.

The opinions expressed in this book are those of the author and do not necessarily reflect the views of the League for Innovation in the Community College.

Requests for permission should be sent to
League for Innovation in the Community College
4505 E. Chandler Boulevard, Suite 250
Phoenix, AZ 85048
email: publications@league.org
Fax: (480) 705-8201

Copies of this book are available through the League's website at www.league.org, or by calling (480) 705-8200.

Printed in the United States of America

378.154 PET 2004

ISBN 1-931300-39-9

Petrides, Lisa Ann, 1961-
Turning knowledge into
action : what's data got

Table of Contents

ACKNOWLEDGMENTS 4

PREFACE 5
Richard N. Katz, Vice President, EDUCAUSE

CHAPTER 1 9
What's Data Got to Do With It?

CHAPTER 2 17
Academic Instruction

CHAPTER 3 31
Supporting Student Learning

CHAPTER 4 45
Supporting a Structure of Inquiry Through Institutional Research

CHAPTER 5 59
Institutional Leadership and Information Use

CHAPTER 6 71
The Impact of External Demands on the Use of Data for Decision Making

CHAPTER 7 85
Informed Decision Making in the Community College

ABOUT THE AUTHOR 99

Acknowledgments

Many individuals have helped to nurture this book into existence. First, I would like to thank those who assisted me in research efforts, from the initial stages of development to final implementation. I am particularly grateful to Thad Nodine and Sara McClelland, who assisted in all stages of protocol design, data collection, analysis, and editing. Additional thanks go to Lilly Nguyen for her research assistance, and to Victoria Manos, the grammar queen. I would especially like to thank Karla Hignite for her editing expertise – for her consistent ability to dive head first into those seemingly elusive passages and transform them with logic and grace.

I would also like to acknowledge the League for Innovation in the Community College, whose enthusiasm and creativity in addressing cutting-edge issues in community colleges appear to know no bounds. In particular, I would like to thank Mark Milliron for his continued support and thought-provoking discussions, Ed Leach for encouraging me to write this book in the first place, and Boo Browning for her patience and editorial guidance.

I am especially grateful to the interviewees who generously gave their time and candidly shared their own successes and challenges in using data, information, and knowledge to improve performance at their colleges. These interviews were enormously useful in helping to shed light on these important and complex issues. I would also like to thank a trusted group of community college advisors for their help in framing the issues contained in these chapters: Katrin Spinetta, Andreea Serban, Barbara Townsend and Harriet Robles. There are many more of you to thank, but not enough room to acknowledge each of you individually.

Lastly, to Mark Graham, whom I neglected to acknowledge last time, a double thank you for your love and support.

Lisa A. Petrides
Half Moon Bay, CA
April 2004

Preface

For more than a decade, scholars and practitioners have written about the "technology paradox," that is, the apparent failure (until quite recently) of our huge investments in information technologies (IT) to have a material impact on economic productivity. Indeed, in higher education, the paradox is even more pronounced, leading some to argue that the instruction and learning processes are magical and therefore exempt from information technology's productivity improvement potential. Such skeptics liken the instructional performance to a concerto and continue the metaphor to argue that seeking productivity is akin to gaining productivity by orchestrating a violin out of a five-piece string ensemble!

And yet we are faced with possibly the greatest conundrum in the history of higher education. To wit: If long-term government support for postsecondary instruction is likely to dwindle over time, and if higher education spending on administrative uses of IT is likely to remain stable or to grow, and if spending on the instructional uses of IT is likely to continue to rise rapidly, what is going to give? In essence, unless higher education begins soon to place IT in the service of real productivity gains, future investments in IT either will be insufficient or will come at the expense of other essential elements of the college experience. A terrible set of choices.

Lisa Petrides provides a great service by illuminating a pathway away from the horns of this particular dilemma. She reminds us that how organizations plan and position themselves for their futures is shaped by the extent to which they understand how raw information is refined into information and ultimately into knowledge that can be used to make decisions and take action.

Higher education in the knowledge-driven era is being reshaped by larger social and political forces:

- The emergence of a postsecondary education as a precondition for effective participation in worldwide labor markets;
- A move away from viewing postsecondary education as a public good to seeing it as a private benefit; and
- The replacement of intellectual and financial capital for land and labor as the dominant factors of economic production.

These broad forces, in turn, have many implications in higher education:

- A growing emphasis on lifelong learning;
- A shift toward a focus on learning outcomes instead of instructional inputs;

- The diminished importance of many political, geographic, and other jurisdictional boundaries that have defined much of the U.S. and European market (*i.e.*, public) for higher education; and
- Increasing calls for transparency and accountability by private and public organizations.

These implications have in common the need for new models, measures, metrics, benchmarks, and tools for assessing and communicating performance – the performance of learners, instructors, and institutions. Like tectonic plates, these implications rub against the IT productivity paradox, demanding our attention in seismic terms.

The need to organize our thinking, our processes, our systems, and our information to turn knowledge into action is clear and present. *Turning Knowledge Into Action* details how the evolving internal pressures for deep understanding of student learning, persistence, and success are conspiring with mounting pressures for accountability and transparency to place a new premium – or even an imperative – on knowledge and decision making. George Keller's celebrated characterization of the academy as a collective of amiable, anarchic scholars with a small cadre of dignified caretakers at the unavoidable business edge can no longer do.[i] Modern colleges and universities, like all social and commercial institutions, are expected to be increasingly adaptable to changing needs in the communities they serve, to be student centered and accountable for their uses of public and customer funds. Muddling through with vague appeals to academic freedom or *in loco parentis* will not withstand the pressures of the knowledge-driven era.

Turning Knowledge Into Action goes well beyond a description of changing environment facing higher education to outline how information technologies can really be placed in the service of student learning. Using powerful frameworks drawn from the emerging field of knowledge management, Petrides describes the potential of community colleges to organize information and technology to yield real-time information that will make it possible to partner with students in previously unimaginable ways toward their mutual goals of academic and developmental success. This book also illustrates how the new complex of information and technology can and must be organized to promote the emergence of a culture of inquiry in the administrative life of the college, and ultimately how such a culture can, must, and will change the very fabric of decision making at all levels of the college.

---

[i] George Keller, *Academic Strategy: The Management Revolution in Higher Education* (Baltimore: Johns Hopkins University Press), 1983.

In the end, Petrides demonstrates how the application of a knowledge management framework can liberate the members of the college community from some of the everyday tyranny of administrivia, freeing faculty and students to pursue their truer purposes. The application of this same framework will also make it possible for college leaders and administrators to manage and guide their organizations more effectively and to account to their stakeholders for their efforts *and* their results.

Turning Knowledge Into Action advocates and describes for its readers a tangible path to organizing and disseminating information within the college in ways that may very well alter the inherent power structures of the institution. The full empowerment of all members of the campus community – where students are the most likely beneficiaries – is the not unspoken agenda of this book.

And what could be a more appropriate agenda for the 21st century community college?

Richard N. Katz
Boulder, Colorado

Chapter 1

What's Data Got To Do With It?

Community college leaders face constant challenges with regard to state budget cuts, changing demographics, and the demand to accommodate a wide variety of students in terms of learning styles, goals, and needs. Because community colleges are increasingly called upon to demonstrate their effectiveness in managing their enterprise and helping students master knowledge and skills, the internal and external drive for improved information about performance puts pressure on community colleges to better manage and promote their institutions. This in turn creates a hunger for more-detailed and contextual information about issues such as student trends. For instance, compared to five years ago, are more students persisting past their first year in college? Are more students completing their programs? Are they being hired by local businesses, and if so, in which industries?

Meanwhile, many academic deans and department chairs, among others, recognize the need to delve deeper into student progress: During the past three years, which groups of students have had the lowest persistence rates? Are certain departments more effective than others in keeping these students enrolled for a second or third year? If so, what practices have made those departments successful in this area?

At the same time, the accountability movement that has spread across the United States has placed additional pressure on higher education institutions to provide reliable results-oriented information (Wells, Silk, & Torres, 1999). In the past, state legislators were content to know how many students were enrolled at a college and how many credits they were taking in which kinds of classes. More recently, however, many legislators are demanding information about the percentage of students who persist past their first year, the percentage who receive certificates and degrees, and the percentage who transfer to four-year institutions. Increasingly, accreditation associations want evidence that data concerning these trends are being gathered and organized into meaningful reports and that the data in these reports are being used in explicit ways to improve student success, not shelved in an obscure storeroom.

Community colleges – particularly hard hit by these new demands for meaningful data from multiple constituencies – must constantly seek new and innovative ways to mobilize their resources toward the efforts these demands entail. Yet despite this widespread emphasis on gathering and using information to improve decision making and performance, many community colleges do not have an adequate way of collecting, using, or analyzing data and information throughout the institution as a whole, let alone an organized process for assessing whether programs, policies, and practices reflect approaches that actually help students succeed.

In many cases, community colleges lack the infrastructure that would provide administrators, faculty, and staff with the information they need. For example, at some institutions, powerful databases are in place that are not integrated and cannot share data between departments. Other community colleges have well-integrated campuswide information systems, but their data can be accessed only by information technology experts who are overworked and do not have time to process requests. Some colleges have enough staff to crunch the numbers but not enough people who can put the data into meaningful contexts. Alternatively, many offices of information technology produce excellent reports, but they are created and distributed too late for the information to be useful. And still other community colleges have implemented new technology systems and web portals to make information available in a timely way to those who need it, yet few people know what is available, know how to use it, or necessarily even want to use it.

Given the fundamental need for appropriate technological processes and systems that can be accessed and administered by the people who need it, it is clear that technology and people are two prime factors that determine how effective a community college ultimately will be in applying data and information to institutional decision making.

The Intersection of People and Technology

Information technology can be a catalyst for bringing transformative change to an organization (Oblinger & Rush, 1997). At its most basic level, the use of technology in an institution often structures the way institutional knowledge is stored and accessed. And there is no doubt that advances in technology contribute significantly to the ways in which higher education organizations provide new opportunities for improved access to and use of information in decision making. However, these technological advances by no means ensure that departments across an academic institution will in fact share information; that the information they do share will be accurate or timely; or that administration, faculty, or staff will use the new tools at their disposal.

Studies have shown that technology tools alone do not address issues of discordant organizational cultures and structures (Telem, 1996; Sirotnik & Burstein, 1987). Studies have also shown that technology itself does not determine the extent to which information is shared and used in decision making within an organizational context (Petrides, 2002; Telem, 1996; Sirotnik & Burstein, 1987). Among the range of factors that can cause a major technology project to fail, few are related to the capability of the technology itself (Johnson & Carney, 2000). Many failed implementations of information systems in higher education have been attributed to the inability of the organizations to improve information sharing and involve multiple users in the creation of knowledge (Leonard & Straus, 1997; Levine, 2001). Not surprisingly, information system failure has also been related to information politics within the organization (Davenport, 1997; Friedman & Hoffman, 2001; Petrides, Khanuja-Dhall, & Reguerin, 2000). And it is often easier to persuade organizations to acquire new technology tools than to modify or redesign existing organizational processes (Coate, 1996).

During the past decade, several states, some community college districts, and many individual community colleges have invested millions of dollars in information technology. What they are finding is that implementing new technology requires a huge organizational shift that can shake institutions to their core, for two primary reasons. First, investments in technology are quite expensive, and advances occur rapidly. Typically, the only single investment that colleges make that is larger than purchases of new technology systems is investment in capital projects. But whereas new buildings and facilities are considered long-term assets with comparatively slow depreciation, large-scale information systems may become outmoded in a decade, and new software and hardware may be obsolete in as little as three or four years. Given the limited financial resources available to community colleges and the rapid changes in technology, community college leaders often delay new technology purchases as long as possible. This often means that when new systems are finally implemented, they require a sudden shift within the organization to accommodate vastly different processes that in turn require intensive retraining of those responsible for using the new systems.

A second reason that technology implementation may result in dramatic organizational change is that effective investment in technology requires new working relationships that cut across traditional organizational and departmental silos. In many cases, department chairs can get approval to purchase office equipment or even hire a new staff position on a case-by-case basis. But the seemingly simple decision to provide a teacher with a new laptop has systemwide implications involving, at the very least, software and hardware compatibility. Likewise, a decision to invest in a new data warehouse system requires major investigation, research, and planning. This entails a systemwide process that necessarily requires lateral communication and problem solving between administrative units such as finance, student services, and enrollment planning – a process that may be uncommon and uncomfortable for many community colleges.

A great number of community colleges do not have extensive track records in bringing together the staff of separate administrative functions to make decisions that affect day-to-day work processes in each department. Moreover, purchasing and implementing new technology often requires extensive vertical communication and problem solving within units. For instance, communication may be required between those who have been the primary users of the old technology – usually lower- and mid-level staff who enter data and order reports from information offices, and those who need access to the information – typically faculty deans and mid- and upper-level managers, many of whom prefer to steer clear of technological details. Sharing information and working both laterally and vertically represents a second significant change in organizational styles for many higher education institutions, and indeed for many organizations outside of higher education as well.

As community colleges work to improve their collection of data, the reporting and sharing of useful information, or the transformation of information into knowledge that can improve performance, technical issues inevitably arise that must be addressed. Unfortunately, the bulk of a manager's time and concerns often focuses on these technical challenges, even though solving them does not resolve the more deeply embedded and systemic organizational issues at stake. While technology and people are the two critical components that determine how successful a community college is in turning institutional data and information into knowledge, people-oriented processes most often present the greater challenge.

The Importance of Human and Organizational Processes

During the past decade, a wealth of research has emerged regarding how to create and share organizational knowledge as well as the relationship between knowledge and organizational change. How organizations plan for their future has been largely shaped by the extent to which they understand the human and organizational processes by which raw data is transformed into useful information, information is internalized as tacit or formal knowledge, and knowledge is used to make decisions and take action. Many have argued that organizations that forge ahead in creating and sharing their most precious resource – knowledge – are those that will be most successful in reaching their goals (Argyris & Schon, 1996; Brown, 1999; Senge, 1990, 1997).

Much of this research is directly applicable to community colleges. For example, Davenport's work on information ecology places primary importance not on technology but on humans, their strategic use of information, and the organization's culture and information politics (Davenport, 1997). This model, which draws on the language of ecology to emphasize holistic systems, suggests that the goals and objectives of an organization can be cultivated simultaneously with the goals and objectives of individuals within it. The ecology metaphor also suggests that the use of knowledge-based information systems requires a framework that mirrors the complexity of community colleges themselves – as active, interdependent, and complex adaptive systems. So what does data have to do with helping institutions transform institutional knowledge into action? Data – collected, analyzed, and appropriately applied – contributes to the successful efforts by institutions and institutional leaders in responding to numerous demands from a variety of audiences. Additionally, the move from strategies for merely handling and distributing data to authentic dialogue about the meaning of that data marks an institution's further progression to the use of knowledge management for continuous learning. By combining technology with inquiry-based decision making, community colleges can take fullest advantage of web-based interfaces, data warehouses, and other information technologies to foster a true culture of inquiry that seeks continuous improvements by instituting a cycle of data collection, analysis, and action.

Toward Informed Decision Making and the Effective Use of Data

Recent developments in organizational change research reveal that effective use of data and information can raise performance, productivity, and outcomes at all levels – for students, faculty, administration, and governance. For instance, community colleges that collect data on student performance, analyze it effectively, and share it in meaningful ways can proactively make decisions about investments in programs and services; they can target remedial assistance promptly to those who need it; they can match course availability with student demand; and they can provide better consumer information for prospective students and other constituents.

More specifically, in teaching and learning, faculty can use classroom-based applications of knowledge management systems in curriculum development, assessment, and course management to facilitate successful course completion for a larger percentage of students. In the area of student services, counselors can use information systems to monitor and track prescribed interventions or use early-alert systems that give counselors the opportunity to respond at the first signs of a potential problem. Likewise, enrollment management can take advantage of online admissions and tracking projected course enrollments based on prior course-taking patterns. Institutional research and planning offices can serve as the nucleus of information in community colleges and facilitate the flow of information throughout the organization. Administration can encourage managers to use data and information for decision making and to ensure that an information-based culture of research and inquiry is in place. And finally, even within the external environment, partnerships with state offices and consortia of information and data users can work together to meet the challenges of state and systemwide accountability and accreditation mandates.

Unfortunately, many community colleges that would like to improve their information systems may be focusing too much of their attention on technical prospects and obstacles. New technology can help to catalyze organizations toward useful change. In realizing that change, however, the more significant challenges are grounded not in technology but in understanding and transforming the organizational culture in which it is embedded.

This book explores how community colleges are facing internal and external pressures regarding efforts to collect, analyze, and share data in ways that lead to proactive decision making. In doing so, this book also examines the organizational challenges that community colleges face as they move toward more-informed decision making. It does so in part by looking at the impact of data, information, and knowledge use in academic instruction and student learning as well as reviewing the role of institutional research and institutional leadership.

These challenges – and some significant solutions – are highlighted by numerous case study examples included throughout the chapters that follow. The examples are based on more than 50 interviews with senior-level administrators at 30 community colleges, including vice chancellors, presidents, vice presidents, deans, program directors, and directors of institutional research. The interviewees represent 18 states across the country and include not only senior-level community college personnel, but also members of state boards, accreditation agencies, and other community college research-related organizations. Because interview participants were guaranteed anonymity as a way to solicit candid responses, pseudonyms are used that portray contextual factors of the colleges and organizations represented, such as the geographic location or size of a college.

Beyond these case studies, no doubt every community college across the country today wrestles with how to get the most from its information systems. Certainly no single road map exists for colleges interested in using better-informed decision making to improve performance. Those who work in a community college know best the financial resources available to them, the information systems they have inherited, their own specific management styles and institutional culture with which they must contend, and how successful their colleges are perceived by outside entities as fulfilling their mission. All these factors affect a community college's ability to effectively engage data for action, and thus its capacity for informed decision making that leads to the continued enhancement of student and institutional success.

References

Argyris, C., & Schon, D. A. (1996). *Organizational Learning II: Theory, Method and Practice.* Redding, CA: Addison-Wesley Publishing Co.

Brown, J. S. (1999). "Sustaining the Ecology of Knowledge." *Leader to Leader,* *12*, 31-36.

Coate, L. E. (1996). "Beyond Re-Engineering: Changing the Organizational Paradigm." In *Organizational Paradigm Shifts.* Washington DC: National Association of College and University Business Offices.

Davenport, T. H. (1997). *Information Ecology: Mastering the Information and Knowledge Environment.* New York: Oxford University Press.

Friedman, D., & Hoffman, P. (2001). "The Politics of Information." *Change,* *33*(2), 50-57.

Johnson, S. L., & Carney, C. (2000). "On the Moving Rock We Stand: Technology and Transition." In M. D. Milliron & C. L. Miles (Eds.), *Taking a Big Picture Look at Technology, Learning, and the Community College* (275-300). Mission Viejo, CA: League for Innovation in the Community College.

Leonard, D., & Straus, S. (1997, July-August). "Putting Your Company's Whole Brain to Work." *Harvard Business Review*, 57-85.

Levine, L. (2001). "Integrating Knowledge and Processes in a Learning Organization." *Information Systems Management, 18*(1), 21-33.

Oblinger, D. G., & Rush, S. C. (1997). *The Learning Revolution: The Challenge of Information Technology in the Academy.* Bolton, MA: Anker Publishing.

Petrides, L. (2002). "Organizational Learning and the Case for Knowledge-Based Systems." In A. Serban & J. Luan (Eds.), *Knowledge Management: Building a Competitive Advantage in Higher Education.* New Directions in Institutional Research, *113*, 69-84. San Francisco: Jossey-Bass.

Petrides, L., Khanuja-Dhall S., & Reguerin P. (2000). "The Politics of Information Management." In L. Petrides (Ed.), *Case Studies of Information Technology in Higher Education: Implications for Policy and Practice* (118-127). Hershey, PA: Idea-Group Publishing.

Senge, P. M. (1990). *The Fifth Discipline.* New York: Doubleday.

Senge, P. M. (1997). "Communities of Leaders and Learners." *Harvard Business Review*, *75*(5), 30-32.

Sirotnik, K. A., & Burstein, L. (1987). "Making Sense Out of Comprehensive School-Based Information Systems: An Exploratory Investigation." In A. Bank & R.C. Williams (Eds.), *Information Systems and School Improvement: Inventing the Future* (185-209). New York: Teachers College Press.

Telem, M. (1996). "MIS Implementation in Schools: A Systems Socio-Technical Framework." *Computers in Education*, *27*(2), 85-93.

Wells, J., Silk, E., & Torres, D. (1999). "Accountability, Technology, and External Access to Information: Implications for IR." In L. Sanders (Ed.), *How Technology is Changing Institutional Research.* New Directions for Institutional Research, *103*, 23-39. San Francisco: Jossey-Bass.

Chapter 2

Academic Instruction

In community colleges, faculty rely on data and information systems to meet a multiplicity of goals, among them: to fulfill the college's mission to ensure that students are successful in meeting their academic goals; to manage the process of academic instruction; and to support innovation and change in their own work environment. For instance, many faculty use email and chat rooms to increase their own availability to students, to enhance their interactions with students, and to increase intellectual interactions among students, all of which may contribute to greater student success. Others use word-processing, spreadsheet, and email applications to improve their productivity in managing classroom instruction, and still others use presentation software to enhance their lectures. Faculty members also use websites and digital documents to complement the resources of their college library.

While more faculty use information technologies to enhance the interactive nature of their curriculum, others use information systems to increase student access to courses through distance education and other means. Green and Gilbert (1995) suggest that increased individual productivity, improved communications, enhanced content, and more interactive curriculum – given supportive organizational settings – are reasonable objectives for campus investment in information technology. Yet, as Green and Gilbert and a host of others have also noted, realizing these kinds of objectives within the decentralized and complex organizational structure of the academic function can be both difficult and expensive. A new question arises: How can information and information technologies be best used by community colleges to take fullest advantage of web-based technologies, information systems, and a culture in which faculty strive to better serve their students?

Most community colleges provide faculty development initiatives in areas such as software applications, assessment methodologies, student outcomes, and interactive curriculum development. These forums can be useful for breaking through the isolation of the classroom, sharing best practices, and promoting a shift to a learning-based curriculum. Yet how might community colleges use ongoing multidisciplinary faculty teams working on assessment to improve student outcomes? Are there ongoing forums for sharing teaching methods from the most experienced master instructors in the college to those with less experience? How much do faculty members, both full- and part-time, know about the demographics of those who have failed their classes? What is the role of information systems in promoting these kinds of knowledge-sharing processes? These are but some of the challenges and opportunities that community college faculty face as they seek to improve the use of information to support student learning.

Assessment of Student Outcomes and Success

During past decades, many faculty members, among others, have sought to transform the academic function at community colleges by making it more student centered. This transformation has been slow in developing, though it is gaining prominence (Schuyler, 1998). A barometer of this transformation is the extent to which faculty members take responsibility for knowing the demographic attributes of their students, understanding student learning styles and outcomes, and tracking student learning based on student-centered tools (Banta, 1999; Barr, 1995).

Many community college faculty are part-time instructors who have multiple teaching assignments. Without the time to analyze student data, they often rely on their intuition to tell them what is successful in the classroom. Even full-time instructors carry heavy courseloads and administrative assignments. On many campuses, collecting and analyzing student data is seen as the job of the program director, the department head, or the dean – not the classroom instructor. Even those instructors who seek better information about student trends, demographics, and outcomes often do not have access to that information. In some cases, the college does not collect the data or has no way of easily extracting it. More commonly, however, extracting data from an information system is possible but requires technological expertise that faculty members often do not have, as well as extensive amounts of time, also in short supply.

At the most basic level, faculty use information systems to access their course lists and grades and obtain limited access to student records. At many colleges, however, faculty do not have direct access to course lists. Subsequently, some faculty do not receive their course lists until the day their class begins, and so there is no way for them to get advance information about the students they will be teaching.

Other community colleges have developed new interfaces with student data so that faculty and administrators can more easily access information that will allow them to make more-informed decisions about the needs of their students. For example, Suburban Coast has implemented a web-based portal, or interface, that gives deans and administrators direct and advance access to class lists as students enroll, with links to information about the enrolled students. The portal also provides an easy way to extract information such as data about the success of students in specific classes or programs. The system was first rolled out for senior-level management and is now used widely by deans and upper management. The next phase of implementation will include training for faculty.

It is important to note that behaviors and norms surrounding data use are often influenced by perceptions of data use in the past, which in turn can influence the time it takes to incorporate ongoing data use as part of current practices. For example, during a 12-month period, Urban West provided faculty with access to a web-based portal that offered similar kinds of information-retrieval capabilities. The college offered faculty training on accessing information through the portal. Yet, because of the ways in which the administrators at the college were perceived as having used data in the past, faculty members remained distrustful of the way data can be manipulated and misunderstood. Therefore, faculty use of the system lagged significantly behind administrative use and well behind projections of system use.

Other community colleges have had greater success in getting faculty to use information made available through web portals, largely because they have invested significant resources in creating a culture where information is used to support instruction and to engage students. In one example, Urban South has been working to make student learning the centerpiece of its enterprise. It has a sophisticated, user-friendly web portal that provides instructors access to course enrollment information and student records and allows them to post their syllabi, assignments, tests, and results online. Through this interface, students can chat with other students, check their grades, and email their instructors. The key to success, at least in part, was that the site was launched through an extensive on-campus marketing campaign. In addition, the college applied for and received a grant that gave reassigned time to 12 different faculty members each fall for several years. During this time, faculty were coached in using the web-based interface and in transforming their curricula to take advantage of its interactive tools. Each spring, these faculty members then trained teams of four to six colleagues from within their departments on how to use the interface.

In another example, Valley Rural College approached faculty access to data and information in a way that not only provided entry to information systems, but also built upon a culture that sought to use information effectively. This was accomplished by developing three levels of information infrastructure. The first level required the implementation of a large enterprise system, a general database that integrates the primary databases throughout the campus. This system, known on campus as "the beast," is considered necessary for bringing together disparate information systems, but it requires extensive time and technical expertise to extract data from it. Because of this, some on campus have come to refer to the new system as "the tail wagging the dog."

The second level of information infrastructure is a series of databases that the institutional research (IR) office maintains and from which longitudinal studies can be performed. Accessing these databases likewise requires technical expertise and a great deal of time. These databases are used primarily for program review.

The third level of information infrastructure is represented by a faculty-level position approved by the faculty senate. The assessment coordinator works with faculty and departments to construct assessment models across the curriculum. According to the dean of instruction, the assessment coordinator has been particularly useful to faculty because she is available to visit classrooms. She assists instructors with assessing the elements of critical thinking that each class develops and in building those components into final papers, projects, or other forms of assessment.

One reason this approach has been successful at Valley Rural is that it is built upon a solid track record of trust among the faculty regarding student assessment. According to the dean of instruction, a multidisciplinary faculty task force focusing on assessment has been operating at the college for more than a decade, and many task force members have attended statewide trainings on assessment and have reported on those workshops to the faculty at large. As a result, faculty members have come to view student assessment across the curriculum as an important internal tool for analysis and support rather than as an external threat to their expertise as instructors. Now, in an ongoing manner, the assessment coordinator works closely with the multidisciplinary task force to continue sharing results across the curriculum.

Other community colleges have likewise developed assessment teams to identify the higher-level thinking and problem-solving skills that students need to master general education courses. Once the skills are defined, these faculty teams assess student work across disciplines and across courses to see how well the students are displaying those skills. At City Midwest, an interdisciplinary faculty committee identified more than a dozen skills critical to success in general education courses. A panel of faculty, counselors, and administrators reviews the skills students exhibit in assignments and tests in capstone courses. In addition, the panel surveys students in classes at all levels about their strengths and weaknesses related to the identified higher-level and problem-solving skills. Based on its findings, the panel makes recommendations for program and curricular improvements.

Student portfolios represent one effective way to assess student achievement and mastery of skills, both within a class and across the curriculum. In the most effective uses of student portfolios, faculty require certain kinds of content and describe specific performance criteria that can be measured objectively, much like an essay assignment would be graded. Often, students are required to write an overview that helps organize the portfolio conceptually. At Mid-South Rural, students put together portfolios of their work in general education courses. Cross-departmental teams of faculty have developed a portfolio-scoring mechanism in four areas – math, culture and ethics, problem solving, and communication – and they apply this scoring mechanism to assess student work (Seybert & O'Hara, 1997).

Electronic portfolios are particularly effective for such interdisciplinary assessments because they facilitate faculty access to student work. For example, students can upload artwork, writing samples, journals, test results, transcripts, community service descriptions, special projects, and other reports and assignments directly to a website or a CD. Faculty can then pull those elements that are most appropriate for their assessment.

In many community colleges, electronic portfolio assessment, if used at all, is often limited to early adopters of technology or to specific departments where the portfolio has real-world applications. For instance, electronic portfolios are popular in the arts, in writing classes, and in business classes because they are portable for the résumé and job-application process. In these cases, electronic portfolios can help raise expectations for both the student and the instructor, since they document student accomplishments and skills and provide an overview of student coursework.

But interdisciplinary assessment and trend analysis of student success, particularly by classroom and department, can be threatening to instructors who are concerned that information may fall into the wrong hands and be used against them. For example, in many instances, questions about student failure rates can fall into a contested zone that is met by silence or dispute about where change should take place.

At Suburban Valley, the dean of learning technologies at the district level was unsuccessful in convincing faculty deans at the colleges about in-class interventions that might help decrease student failure rates. She was particularly concerned about algebra since, as she claimed, more than half of the students fail the subject and many students fail two or three times. She met with division deans to discuss the situation and proposed some technologically interactive learning modules to improve test scores. When asked how much she was going to pay the deans to do this work, she interpreted the question as a reaction to her encroaching on their territory – district intrusion into a college matter, and administrative invasion of an area of faculty expertise. She decided to let the issue go, and nothing has since been done.

There are, however, plenty of examples of faculty at community colleges working with the administration and with student services to improve student results. In many cases, faculty are prompting the administration to get better data so that improvements can more effectively be targeted to student needs. For instance, math faculty at Southeastern Metro, concerned about their department's high failure rate, worked with the college IR office to examine differences in completion rates based on several possible variables, such as by campus, by teacher, according to the prerequisites of the student, and whether the teacher was adjunct or full-time. Based on the results, faculty learned that course sequencing and student placement were problematic. In particular, students who placed directly into a higher-level math course did not perform as well as those who had initially placed into lower-level courses. This analysis provided the department the information it needed to adjust course sequencing and to monitor its progress.

English faculty at another community college, Tri-State South, found that certain demographic groups were failing courses in higher numbers than were other groups. As a result, they developed interventions to meet student instructional needs. In each of these examples, both administration and faculty had invested time and resources in using information effectively in decision making. The faculty were comfortable that the results of the research efforts would be directed toward improvements and not toward punitive measures that might decrease the resources necessary to address the issues.

Another indicator of student success to many community colleges is that of student enrollment and retention. At Middletown Metro, faculty input was used to improve the accuracy of a newly developed student enrollment database. The database, which tracks enrollment over time, is available online to deans, who share information with faculty in their departments. While it took a full year of working with interdepartmental committees for the IR office to attend to all the complaints and recommendations regarding the database, the ease of the online interface has for the first time made it possible for deans to run reports themselves, allowing them to compare and track enrollment levels for specific programs, sections, and majors. One outcome is that deans and many faculty have become much more interested in making sure that the data about their departments is accurate and current.

A second, unexpected outcome was that the implementation of the enrollment database led to initiating the development of a student retention database. This database, which will track completion and retention, is being developed by the IR office and will be available online. While there has been faculty resistance to the retention database, faculty participation in implementation of the enrollment database and widespread agreement about the accuracy of its data have helped garner trust among the faculty and deans. Without the development of the enrollment database, the retention database likely would not have been possible.

In addition, administrators at Middletown Metro were able to generate faculty support for the gathering of classroom data by applying for and receiving a federal grant that required tracking student progress, monitoring outcomes, and then using the information to create interventions outside the classroom. The college hired a half-time staff person to track student success in several areas, and a faculty and staff committee was immediately formed to design a student database that would function outside the limited capabilities of the college's student information system. A student success database was created that generates an electronic roster sent to each instructor. Faculty members fill out the roster for the students in their classes, suggesting interventions such as tutoring for students who need additional help. The information is sent to the staff at the academic support center, which generates a letter to the student concerning the intervention.

While funding for this project has since run out, the student tracking database continues to be used with support from the faculty. As faculty members have gathered information, placed it within appropriate contexts, and generated clarifying questions, they have become more comfortable with having the college compile data and are more willing to engage in discussions about its use for analysis and improvement. In fact, now that faculty are in the habit of accessing student trend information, many welcome its use for innovations that will improve student outcomes. The use of the student tracking database has also increased collaboration and exchange of information between faculty and academic support staff.

Interaction in the Web-Enhanced Classroom

No doubt, information technologies have the potential to transform the way the classroom operates. This is true not only for distance education classes, but also for traditional classrooms that include elements of web-based technologies. Faculty members who gain experience with the capabilities of information technology often use these technologies to transform their traditional courses. At Upstate Metro, where most faculty reportedly are adept with information technologies, faculty have come to rely heavily on technology as a communication device in their teaching and research. Of 240 full-time faculty, more than 25 percent have developed full online courses, and an additional 25 percent have supplemented their courses with web-based or online components. In the health department, for example, all exams and tutorials are online.

According to faculty surveys and anecdotal evidence at Upstate Metro, the introduction of online elements has changed what instructors do in the classroom in several ways. First, the use of email and chat rooms in courses has changed the way the instructors communicate with students and has increased student-teacher interactions by increasing the amount of contact that many students now have with their instructors. As part of their class assignments, students are often required to post messages and otherwise participate in online discussion groups. Whereas in traditional classroom discussions there generally is not enough time for everyone to participate, in online discussions the instructor can require every student to answer certain questions. Used in this way, the electronic venue can increase participation levels, and has in fact done so.

Second, faculty have found that when students are required to do online research, they have far more access to external materials that can enrich and provide context for course content. Some instructors of agriculture, after teaching several online courses, decided they would require students in their traditional classes to get direct access to and explore the state department of agriculture's online products. Students were required to visit websites, learn about topics such as crop maturation, and attend class ready to discuss the pertinent issues. In the traditional classroom setting, instructors brought that kind of information to class. Requiring students to access materials directly made the classroom discussions more lively and interactive, and students often added insights about information they had discovered on their own.

Third, faculty in some departments at Upstate Metro found that having online access to each other changed how they worked together. For instance, each year in the English department, a group of faculty would sit down in a room to grade writing-placement essays of incoming freshmen. During these meetings, they would compare essays and their grades to make sure their grading was consistent from one instructor to the next. Today, essays are all available online, and the instructors are also meeting online. They are finding that it is easier to track and reference the kinds of student writing that receive one grade versus another from one year to the next. By creating an online, formalized, organizational memory of their work, they do not have to reinvent their grading criteria each year. The next step will be to create a search engine that will sort how instructors responded to certain kinds of writing – for instance, examples of punctuation errors, subject-verb agreement, or paragraph form. Online access to other faculty encouraged all to work more collaboratively than they had in the past and allowed new patterns of work to emerge.

Several years ago, City South Community College invested significant resources to create a laptop campus. Essentially, each student was required to pay a technology fee for which the student received a laptop for use during the year. Students in wired classrooms brought their laptops to class and hooked up during class time. However, due to the high cost of the program for both the college and the students, the college ultimately eased this requirement and is now in the process of determining which classes or programs will continue to compel student access to laptops.

Although City South is still collecting data to assess the impact of laptops in classrooms on student outcomes, several surveys documenting student and faculty use of and satisfaction with the program suggest that many classroom activities have been transformed as a result of the availability of the laptops for in-class and out-of-class work. Specifically, English faculty reported that student access to laptops facilitated student editorial feedback on peer essays. For some time, many English instructors required students to edit each other's essay drafts in class before submitting a final version of the essay to the instructor. Since everyone had access to laptops, this process could be done electronically. Students emailed each other their papers and inserted their editorial suggestions as comments attached to their peers' manuscripts.

Among other supportive findings, history faculty reported that the interactive software made available by the laptops brought to life the dynamics of the historical time period they teach in ways that written materials previously had not. One instructor reported that the students' own writing became more vivid and engaging as a result. Likewise, science faculty found that interactive software transformed the laptops into three-dimensional laboratories. In chemistry, for instance, software not only presented students with three-dimensional graphics showing the makeup of molecules, but also enabled students to combine molecules and witness their transformation. In addition, students could change the temperature and then recombine the molecules to see how temperature change affected the experiment.

At Suburban Valley, many faculty who have infused web-based elements into their classes have realized the need to reconsider their subject content as well as their teaching styles. An English instructor added chat sessions, email, and extensive student-to-student writing assignments to her basic writing course, English 1A. As she added these online elements, she found that she was not only working with students on basic grammar and style, but also engaging them in a new kind of online writing style that was more immediate and more student centered. She found that students communicated with each other much more frequently than they had in previous classes. She also found that whereas students in traditional courses tended to write the minimum amount required, students participating in online writing formats wrote much more than they were asked to write. Although she did not have quantitative data to back it up, anecdotally the instructor felt that the class was more successful than it had ever been. She also believed that one reason students were writing better is that they were writing for each other; they knew their peers would read their work online.

Use of information technology offers a world of opportunities to track specific student actions, activities, and assignments. These elements may include the number of postings in a class chat room, a record of a student's online interactions with other students, the number of peer essays that a student has downloaded, or the length of time spent on a class website or engaged in internet research. Each of the community colleges mentioned has been at the forefront of introducing online or virtual elements in traditional class settings and implementing nontraditional online teaching and learning environments. In addition to completing surveys of faculty and student use of online tools, some faculty members in limited situations at each of these community colleges have attempted to track how often students were using the web or how many times students accessed class websites during the semester to get a rough picture of student activity on the web. These colleges were also very interested in the extent to which online offerings expanded their enrollments and increased access to higher education to those who might not otherwise be able to participate. In general, however, there has been much less effort invested in studying student success or failure in relation to online offerings, and it appears that this potential use of information technology remains largely untapped.

Support of Faculty Collaboration and Innovation

Organizations that promote effective exchange of information among their principal stakeholders are likely to improve their chances of engaging these strategic groups in helping them reach their most important goals and objectives (Davenport, 1997). Specifically, the ways in which a community college supports collaboration and innovation are intrinsically linked to the ways in which it provides its members with timely access to data that supports continuous improvement (Banta, 1999). While the implementation of information technology can prompt faculty to work together to achieve these goals effectively, this is not always the case. In fact, concerted efforts made by the college are what most often allow these institutions to meet their improvement goals.

Many community colleges have created technology advisory committees composed of faculty, administrators, students, staff, and others. For example, Upstate Metro found this kind of ongoing task force very useful in breaking down barriers to technology use within faculty departments. Since every faculty department has representation on the college's technology panel, each has a voice in crucial purchasing and implementation decisions. This approach helps put a human face on campuswide technology decisions. Equally important, the responsibility for communicating technological issues to the departments rests with department faculty rather than with the information technology (IT) department.

When Upstate Metro learned that one of its vendors of interactive course management software was raising its price prohibitively, the administration, knowing that faculty were already trained to use the software, brought the issue before the technology committee. The panel worked with IT staff to consider other software options and then tested those options and provided feedback. According to the director of learning initiatives, having an ongoing task force is very different from calling together ad hoc committees or making a presentation to the faculty senate. Because the task force has been a permanent committee, it has educated the faculty about technological purchasing and implementation and has built trust and credibility among faculty regarding technological issues.

City Southeast developed a state-of-the-art distance learning system that brought its degree and certificate programs to several thousand students solely through web-based distance education. The interactive online technology expanded access to students by allowing flexibility in scheduling and instruction of courses. During the past several years, the program has seen enormous enrollment growth. Although no data have been gathered yet with regard to student retention or satisfaction, the program has collected survey data from online faculty. According to survey results, online faculty felt uninformed about what services were available to students. As a result, program administrators implemented training to provide online faculty with a brief introduction to the services available on campus so they would have the necessary information to answer students' questions about accessing student services.

There were, as well, other significant ways in which online faculty were not brought together with campus faculty. In curriculum development, for example, new campus faculty who were scheduled to teach established courses were assigned mentors who had taught the courses in the past. Online faculty developed their courses on their own, and no such collaboration was encouraged. Not surprisingly, online faculty reported feelings of isolation from the campus as a whole, from campus faculty, and from each other. Subsequently, there has been little interest among online faculty in collecting and analyzing data about student demographics or outcomes, thereby leaving it to the marketing department to actively pursue demographic data. Similarly, online faculty are not using electronic student portfolios or other forms of cross-disciplinary assessment, even though the vast majority of assignments and tests is available electronically.

At the other end of the spectrum, Urban Central District, whose colleges have extensive course offerings in distance education and web-based technologies, has taken a very proactive approach to the sharing of information among faculty and departments on each campus. Several years ago, this district used grant funding to hire a chief knowledge officer (CKO) in charge of evaluating and enhancing, on a campus-by-campus basis, the extent to which various campus units built on and formalized their knowledge base.

On the one hand, the district was concerned that its own existing processes were out of date and overly bureaucratic. On the other hand, it was concerned that in many areas, campus units did not have formal processes in place for maintaining and enhancing organizational memory. For instance, if a principal individual retired, would the college have to reinvent certain crucial processes? The new CKO completed a knowledge audit in which she asked administrators, staff, and faculty members about the essential information they needed regularly and about those college or district processes that were especially time-consuming and bothersome. Each participant was viewed as an expert in a respective area. The audit was used not only to help gather information, but also to help staff and faculty realize that their duties could be made easier if their expertise was shared and certain processes streamlined.

The CKO began working with existing task forces and committees to transform them into communities of practice (CoPs). The idea was to harness existing organizational energy to formalize and streamline college procedures. The chairs of the existing task forces became knowledge coordinators. Each CoP was organized tightly around specific functions, and the members began working to identify the knowledge that needed to be shared for their functions to be successful, to identify areas and procedures that were preventing success, and to outline the steps required to improve work processes in those areas.

Faculty were particularly frustrated by the curriculum development process, which they viewed as so bureaucratic, inflexible, and time-consuming that they were convinced the college was losing enrollment to other institutions that were developing and offering new courses more expeditiously. As a result, a CoP was developed to improve the curriculum development process. Several faculty members participated along with academic counselors and several administrators. The committee mapped the workflow process for developing and getting approval for new curriculum, including identifying the offices that needed oversight, the information they needed, research requirements regarding best practices, and approval timelines.

At about this time, the grant funding ended and the district decided to institutionalize the position of CKO. That decision, combined with the work of the curriculum development CoP, enhanced the influence of the CKO among faculty on campus. Prior to that, many faculty believed that since the position was grant funded, it was not worth sharing what they knew. Over time, however, faculty began to trust the work of the CKO and saw that the position did bring improvements to their work environment.

Meanwhile, the interim coordinator of the curriculum development CoP left the college, and another faculty participant was on the brink of retirement. This provided all the more reason to develop processes to formalize organizational memory. After taking a year to map workflow, the institution is preparing to implement software that promises to streamline and monitor the curriculum development approval process. During that year, faculty came together to create a ground-up implementation to replace what they had considered a burdensome, top-down mandate.

The Potential to Transform

Many community college faculty are interested in obtaining better data and information about student outcomes and student success. For a variety of reasons, however, many colleges do not provide instructors with basic information about student success rates and trends. Faculty members are using technological advancements in communications and teaching to improve and increase student-faculty and student-student interactions. Many instructors have used electronic portfolios and other means for assessing student skill levels within and across disciplines. The use of these kinds of tools has the potential to transform the way faculty share knowledge with each other and with their students.

Yet without better and more readily available information about student outcomes, there is no guarantee that electronically mediated course materials, no matter how interactive, are any more effective than traditional teaching methods. In fact, they may be less so in specific situations and in relation to certain demographic groups. The issue is not whether faculty are using information technology in the classroom or to support their students, but how they use it, how they share their knowledge with other faculty members, and what impact their teaching and their use of information technology is having on student outcomes. If that kind of information is not available from the college, the crucial question looms: Are students being served most effectively, and how can we know for sure?

References

Banta, T. W. (1999). *Assessment in Community Colleges: Setting the Standard for Higher Education?* Boulder, CO: National Center for Higher Education Management Systems.

Barr, R. B. (1995). "From Teaching to Learning: A New Reality for Community Colleges."*Leadership Abstracts, 8*(4). Last accessed: December 23, 2003, from http://www.league.org/publication/abstracts/leadership/labs0395.htm.

Davenport, T. H. (1997). *Information Ecology: Mastering the Information and Knowledge Environment.* New York: Oxford University Press.

Green, K., & Gilbert, S. (1995). "Great Expectations: Content, Communications, Productivity, and the Role of Information Technology in Higher Education." *Change, 27*(2), 8-18.

Schuyler, G. (1998). *A Paradigm Shift from Instruction to Learning.* Los Angeles, CA: ERIC Clearinghouse for Community Colleges. Last accessed: October 3, 2002, from www.gseis.ucla.edu/ERIC/digests/dig9802.html.

Seybert, J. A., & O'Hara. (1997). "Development of a Performance-Based Model for Assessment of General Education." *Assessment Update, 9*(4), 5-7.

Chapter 3

Supporting Student Learning

The concept of student success in the community college has had multiple definitions and measures over time. Student success has often been defined in terms of the achievement of the institution as a whole, such as an increase in access and equity measures. More recently, with the advent of accountability mandates, it has been defined as the number of degrees or certificates conferred by the institution. Over time, success also has been defined in terms of how effective students have been in the achievement of their own goals, such as persistence and completion (Astin, 1982; Ender et al., 1996). This range of definitions and measures of student success is reflective of the protean missions that community colleges serve: workforce training and retraining, basic skills building, and academic transfer, to name a few. It also connects the disparate functions of a complex educational institution to the aspirations of individual students pursuing their own educational needs.

Serving these multiple student agendas complicates the task of the community college in achieving its objectives. Under the framework of helping students achieve their own educational goals, the success of students can no longer be measured simply by institutional success (*i.e.*, the number of certificates and degrees conferred). If a college is focused on improving student success, then college personnel and resources are brought to bear to help the student assess educational goals, adjust them where needed, and monitor progress toward them, as well as to provide students the means to reach their goals. To attain these ends, many colleges are transforming their information systems and information culture to engage students more actively in their own educational and career planning and to connect them to the academic support services they need, both on campus and online.

Using Information Technology to Support Student Learning

Educational planning offers community colleges a significant opportunity to record student goals, monitor progress toward achievement of them, and engage students in one of the essential educational functions of the college: the overall development of the whole student. The student service function fills a central role in supporting student learning in the community college. Student learning services span a range of activities, from helping students develop educational plans that align with their personal and professional goals to counseling that enables them to meet the challenges of pursuing higher education and lifelong learning. New information technologies have allowed community colleges to develop a better understanding of the needs and desires of their students as well as to deploy some of the more traditional student services with a new interactive component.

Traditionally, community colleges have had a process in place by which students fill out the equivalent of an educational plan that includes a planned program of study as well as a timeline of courses necessary to finish the particular program. While many colleges require incoming students to complete educational plans, some do not have effective systems to monitor student progress in relation to those plans. For instance, at Suburban West, located in a state that requires matriculating students to complete educational plans, the college does not track whether students do in fact have an educational plan in place. Students fill out the plans as part of a 12-hour orientation class for incoming first-year students that is offered in a variety of formats, including online. However, most freshmen do not take the class during their first semester, and many never do. When students do fill out educational plans at this particular college, they do so on paper, and the plans are never entered into a database. As a result, no automated means exists for monitoring aggregate student progress in relation to their plans. Likewise, even individual efforts to monitor a student's success are difficult. It is not uncommon for a student to fill out one educational plan during the orientation course, a second upon visiting the academic counseling office, and a third with a different counselor a year later.

In this situation, educational planning may be helping some or perhaps many students to connect their aspirations to the actual course opportunities at the college, but it offers no effective way to help students stay on course or develop alternatives if their career plans change. In addition, this haphazard approach makes it difficult for the college to assess whether it is succeeding in meeting student objectives since it has no means for compiling the data over time.

Other community colleges gather initial information about student intention on an application form but then either do not ask for student educational goals or do not use that information later to determine whether a student's initial goal is in line with actual class-taking patterns. For example, Northwest Metro requires students to answer a question on their application forms concerning their intentions for attending the college, but the college has no requirement for students to complete a more-detailed educational plan. On the application, students are merely asked their primary reason for attending the college and can select from several general answers (*e.g.*, to improve their reading and writing skills, to pursue a degree). Additionally, the student's declaration of overall intent does not take into account skill levels or transcript information, and it is not aligned with any particular course-taking patterns.

Some community colleges that have implemented information systems to assist students in meeting their goals have done so without fully considering the range of unintended consequences that could result from putting those systems in place. For example, West Rural College, which is part of the West Rural Community College District, implemented a relational database used to require first-year students to complete educational plans. It decided to block first-time students from registering for their second semester if they did not have an educational plan on file. However, when the college first implemented the registration-blocking system, many students who were not first-year students were incorrectly blocked from registration. The college had to remove the blocking system for a semester until certain technical procedures were implemented that could better identify first-year students. While the system is now labeling students correctly, counselors have felt overburdened by the number of students being sent to them for one-on-one sessions to create an educational plan. Many counselors think the educational planning should be handled through group orientation sessions rather than one-on-one meetings, and that larger discussion is still under way.

Similarly, one urban high-growth college, Northwest Metro, has experienced 22 consistent quarters of growth, increasing its annual enrollment from 10,000 to 18,000 students during the past four years. Counselors have seen new faculty members hired to teach the additional students, but within those four years there have been no increases in the number of academic counselor positions. The student demand for one-on-one academic counseling is so high that counselors feel completely overburdened and stressed. At a recent planning meeting, the counselors agreed that retention rates would improve if all students completed educational plans. Yet when they discussed implementing such a requirement, they decided to table the issue since they could not see themselves absorbing the increased workload that would inevitably result.

As these examples illustrate, a common result of implementing an information system is that it can raise issues that the organization had not previously anticipated. Whether, for instance, educational plans should be developed in one-on-one meetings or in orientation sessions is a valid question that must be resolved by each organization. And while the participation of staff in these discussions is a sign of attempts to effectively manage information processes, these basic questions can go unearthed until after a new information system is already designed and implemented.

At the other end of the spectrum is a college where these types of discussions are taking place not only among administrators, but also between faculty and administrators, thereby helping to bridge academic and support services. At East Metro, students define their goals on their student applications, which in turn triggers significant educational planning, including academic counseling, early-alert systems, and access to other support services, many of them online. The questions on the application are detailed, inquiring about the student's academic program and level of certainty about the chosen program and career field, grades expected, plans to transfer or enter the job market, and whether the student needs assistance with financial aid, child care, career planning, or other areas that could affect the student's ability to complete educational goals.

This information and the student's placement test results are entered into a database that creates an online educational plan for the student. The information system is accessible electronically by the academic advisor as well as the student. Each student who declares a major is paired with an advisor in the appropriate department. Students who do not declare are paired with an academic counselor from student affairs. Every student is required to meet with an advisor or counselor during the first semester. Some academic programs require students to continue meeting with their advisors each term; other programs do not require additional meetings but do require student-advisor contact if students are not progressing toward their goals.

East Metro can also monitor the progress of any group, such as those who have not declared a major or those who checked a need for assistance in a particular area. For instance, the "career undecided" group is offered assistance in career planning. After a set period of time, those who have not declared a major receive a letter asking them to meet with a counselor to discuss interests and options.

East Metro's system has helped students connect their overall goals with specific courses of study. When application questions about educational planning were first developed and implemented, the college was able for the first time to track student success in relation to goals. Yet the results were not always favorable. The college found that many students were dropping out of their selected educational plans. East Metro responded by convening a task force that included faculty, staff, and students to explore the functional issues with the system, consider the results obtained, and make recommendations for improvement. The task force learned that the original questions on the application were too general and that the information students provided was often misleading. For example, many students filled in "computers" for their field of interest, but that could mean anything from computer programming to learning how to use a specific software application.

Based on the task force's findings, student affairs staff met with department chairs to discuss options. As a result of this process, the college made the application questions more specific and provided additional front-loaded services to students, including additional screening that supplied certain answers. In the year after East Metro implemented these changes, overall student retention rates increased by more than 7 percent.

In the case of East Metro, implementation of an information system did not by itself improve student performance, but it did offer the college opportunities it previously did not have to monitor student outcomes and to work across disciplines and across departments to improve results. It was, in fact, the interactions across disciplines and departments that were directly responsible for the improvements. It is also important to note that these changes took place within a college culture that was already very outcomes-oriented.

Several years earlier, East Metro's president had spearheaded a campuswide strategic "vision for excellence" that emphasized the use of data tools, focus groups, survey information, and other internal monitoring devices to improve services to students. Within this campus culture, the development of online student resources and support services was accomplished by convening a cross-functional task force jointly chaired by the vice president of academic affairs and the vice president of student services. The task force was composed of faculty, department chairs, coordinators of student services, and IT specialists. Because the college had different program areas involved in designing the system from the start, the system was viewed not as the specialty of either academic affairs or student affairs, but as the responsibility of both. Within this context, individuals tended to regard any problems that arose as challenges for the entire campus rather than as the fault of a specific unit.

Responding to Implementation Challenges

As more community colleges are stepping forward with innovative ways to support the success of their students, some are combining more traditional methods with new web-based applications while others are developing new cross-disciplinary models to engage students, faculty, and student service providers. All of these implementations face challenges along the way – some of them unanticipated. Two examples of new information systems implementation illustrate the ways in which student services, as part of the larger college culture, faced these challenges and how they used what they learned during the design and implementation process to further support student success.

One example is West Rural, a midsize community college with three separate campuses. While students enrolled at the college are allowed to take courses at any of the campuses, they are assigned to one campus, with their records maintained at the assigned campus. In part because of the decentralization of student information on the three campuses, the college's ability to monitor student educational plans and keep track of which advisors students have seen has been problematic at best. For instance, if a student assigned to one campus visited a counseling office at another campus, that counseling office did not have access to the student's files.

To promote better information exchange among its three campuses, West Rural decided to convert, through electronic scans, all paper files of educational plans, transcripts, and other student documents. The process was described by one of its chief proponents as "a nightmare" and "a time hog," but one that would eventually save a great deal of time. In developing the system, the college hired a vendor to scan all the documents it planned to convert. The first vendor hired did not deliver on promises and was unable to complete the job. The second vendor converted several hundred thousand documents, only to determine that the new files could not be tied into the college's new information system. The college then purchased another software program to convert these files into usable documents that their information system could read.

Now that the conversion process is almost completed, college personnel and academic counselors at all three campuses have access to hundreds of thousands of student documents, or more precisely, pictures of the documents. The new system allows students the flexibility to seek academic counseling from whichever campus they choose, thereby preventing a student from having to travel between campuses to take advantage of academic counseling services.

However, the new system does not have the capability to convert the scanned documents into recognizable characters. As a result, the information cannot at this time be entered automatically into a database that can be queried based on the fields of information found in the transcripts and other records. Significant improvements in the use of information are still lacking, and the problem is further complicated by broader organizational difficulties. Because the state itself has not standardized transcript information, course titles and numbering systems vary widely among its colleges. Even more critically, baccalaureate colleges and universities disagree on which courses are acceptable for credit. This makes the conversion from optical image to a database that can be manipulated and queried that much more problematic. Until agreement is reached on these issues, no easy way exists to create a technological solution that can translate transcripts into a standard format. This piece of the puzzle must wait for statewide action, though perhaps development and implementation of these kinds of information systems will provide impetus for the state systems of higher education to agree on a uniform course-transfer policy and numbering system.

Reflecting on the process used to implement the scanning system, West Rural administrators felt that one useful alternative would have been to start small, *i.e.*, to establish a pilot project with the aim of converting one kind of document for a set number of students. These results could then have been evaluated before moving forward, gradually instituting changes in stages. Other colleges have rolled out new information systems in this way, allowing them to maintain their existing technology until successes with the new system were visible.

A second example involves a different information technology: online counseling. At East Metro, the decision to offer online counseling entailed implementing a system that would allow students to communicate with counselors in real time via chat sessions. This meant students would not have to physically visit an office or wait in line to meet with a counselor in person. Initially, counselors were distrustful of the technology, suspecting it would be more time consuming for them than actually talking with students face to face. They also thought it would be too impersonal for effective counselor-student relationships.

The associate dean of matriculation who spearheaded the efforts in this arena had a history of working with technology, was acutely aware of its limits, and understood the distrust the counselors held toward it. To implement the system, the dean established a pilot project for which she sought a group of five counselors who were generally experienced with using computers and who were open to the opportunities of the online technology. The dean believed it was important to include one counselor opposed to the technology but who was professional about his job and could be fair in his assessment. In addition, the online sessions would be made available only to students who were taking courses online, ensuring that they would already be familiar with this particular technology.

As expected, during the pilot project, the counselors who were less familiar with technology and computers in general were apt to become more frustrated by how long the sessions took, with the pace of their own typing, or when students would get bumped off the system or would otherwise seem to disappear, thereby disrupting the online counseling session. Over time, however, counselors learned that they could pick up the phone and call the student or email the student to say that they were still online and would remain so for a set number of minutes to answer any questions. Overall, the counselors found the technology very useful because it reached students who were not generally inclined to visit the office. The feedback from students was even more positive, demonstrating that they found the service convenient and helpful.

When the project was ready to be extended to all the counselors, the associate dean relied on those who had participated in the pilot to relate their experiences to the initiates. As a way to garner support for the project, she distributed information about the student body's use of and familiarity with computers and their proclivity to go online for services and products. She presented the new service as another way for students to receive counseling rather than as a new service that the college was providing. Her objective was to make the transition to this new technology as seamless as possible for the counselors.

Although a host of concerns have surfaced among counselors as they have tried to learn the new technology, by and large the implementation has been successful, providing a way for students taking online classes to access academic counseling without having to drive to campus. The counselors who participated in the pilot project have been helpful in convincing other counselors of the merits of the system. Counselors have since reported that during their online sessions, students tend to stay on task much more effectively, with little time wasted discussing the weather and other irrelevant issues. In addition, the new technology has prompted useful discussions among counselors about the nature and the limits of counseling in both face-to-face and electronic settings.

As with the conversion of paper documents to electronic files at West Rural, some significant opportunities that could have resulted from the new online counseling technology at East Metro may have been missed. For instance, by presenting the system to counselors as nothing new – as simply another way for students to access counseling services – the dean may have made implementation of the new service smoother. On the other hand, by not brainstorming with counselors beforehand about the new technology, the college may have missed an opportunity to reach new levels of performance, such as tailoring services to a different group of students.

For example, in offering online chat sessions, East Metro uses technology effectively to increase the availability of an important service. However, the college does not log or save the transcripts of these sessions. In part, this is a consequence of the technology used, but another reason is that counselors did not want the transcripts of these sessions on record. As a result, no basic protocols were developed for later data retrieval. Yet, because online sessions are already text files, they offer opportunities for data queries, outcome assessment, quality improvement, and data mining that reach well beyond what a personal encounter would make available. But if the information from the text files is not saved, these opportunities are lost.

Engaging Students in Their Own Success

Community colleges are using information technologies to engage students in taking a more active role in their own educational and career planning throughout their college experience. Degree-audit systems, early-alert systems, academic-related interventions, and developmental advising are examples of the information systems being used for this purpose. In addition, some colleges have developed web-based portals or information systems that enable students to perform certain functions online, such as viewing grades, completing surveys on life and career goals, finding out about degree requirements, and creating and updating education plans.

One way colleges have used information systems to engage students in educational planning is with degree-audit systems that allow students to update their educational plans in relation to the courses they have taken and their current educational goals. Suburban West recently received a grant to develop a new online system to allow students to complete degree audits on their own and to determine what courses they would need if they decided to switch majors or if they wanted to transfer to a different community college or a baccalaureate institution.

Suburban West began by developing a pilot program and having counselors test the system. In the process, the college encountered significant problems stemming from a lack of communication within the institution. Several departments within the college had revised their requirements without communicating these changes to the IT specialists who were programming the new degree-audit system. One department revised its numbering system without informing the programmers. To make matters worse, the programmers were not told explicitly that the requirements pertaining to each student were the ones that were valid the year that student entered the college. As a result of these communication lapses, the counselors uncovered numerous errors. Because they had questions about the accuracy of the information, some counselors performed both an automated and a paper degree audit and compared the two. Many have since lost faith in the new system altogether. The system, while unsuccessful in its pilot form, is more a reflection of organizational gnarls than the result of a technical glitch, and it underscores the importance of working cross-functionally on campuses.

An example of a successfully implemented pilot program is seen within West Rural Community College District, which developed an early-alert system during the course of a two-year period to connect students with services that could help them complete their courses successfully. The task force in charge of planning for this early-alert system brought together faculty members and student services personnel. The system was piloted in the math department on one campus and then extended to math teachers districtwide. Following the pilot phase, the system was expanded to the sciences and is now in effect for all academic programs.

Under the early-alert system, faculty are given forms to fill out during the fourth or fifth week of classes to identify students who are in danger of failing a class. For those students selected, faculty indicate whether they recommend (1) a visit to the tutoring center, (2) a meeting with the faculty member, or (3) a visit with an academic counselor. Based on the professor's recommendations, that college automatically sends out letters to students. It remains the student's responsibility to initiate contact with the tutoring center, the professor, or a counselor. Some students who are upset when they receive these letters express their displeasure to their professors by coming to see them in person. This is actually seen as one sign of the success of the system in that it is prompting more communication between professors and students about the students' work.

Several colleges across the country are developing and implementing online interactive tools that build on the concept of developmental advising, a student-centered process that assists students in identifying and clarifying their educational goals within the context of their interests, abilities, and background experiences. Developmental advising encourages students to consider broader questions about life and career goals and then helps them develop and update a shorter-term educational plan within those long-term frameworks (Frost, 1991). In this context, developmental advising enhances student interaction with the college, enabling students to become more integrated in the learning experiences that shape college life (Astin, 1984; Pisani & Stott, 1998).

In one example, Urban South received a grant to implement a new information system of support within a developmental advising framework. The design and implementation of these tools brought together faculty and staff. The college's efforts in this area grew from a culture that was willing to admit dissatisfaction with student results. It had already begun to track the progress of degree-seeking students and found that too few of these students completed certificates or degrees. Urban South also acknowledged that students needed general guidance in understanding their own learning styles, experiences, and career goals, and that the already overburdened academic counseling office did not have the means to get this information and these resources to students.

Based on results from student focus groups, Urban South discovered that students come to career and educational planning from one of four primary perspectives: (1) They have a good idea of what degree they are seeking but are not certain of the career that might interest them. (2) They have a good idea of the career that interests them but do not know which degree path would be best for them. (3) They have a good idea of their career goals and an accurate degree plan for getting there. (4) They are not certain of their career or degree goals.

Working together in teams, staff and faculty identified and focused on five primary transition stages for students, and they developed information and resources that students would need to be successful at each of those stages: (1) the high school transition, (2) introduction to college, (3) progress toward the degree, (4) graduation and transfer, and (5) career development. A web portal was developed with tools available for each of those stages and with links to college offices that could help in each transition. The online interfaces were designed to help students connect their long-term career goals with their shorter-term educational goals.

Meanwhile, about a dozen faculty members were provided with reassigned time each fall to learn the concepts of developmental advising, to learn about the new online tools available, and to bring active learning strategies into their classrooms. In the spring term, each of these faculty members worked with four to six colleagues within their departments to discuss the use of online tools both in the classroom and in advising students.

At the beginning, faculty members voiced opposition to assuming an advising role. As they viewed it, they had, and still have, no contractual obligation to advise, and there was already a professional, albeit overburdened, advising staff on campus. But over time, the faculty training, combined with the faculty's teamwork with staff members in developing the online services, helped to change this mindset. As faculty learned more about the online tools and the counseling resources available to students, they felt more comfortable discussing these elements with their students both inside and outside of class.

The online resources were pilot tested prior to their release, and when they were ready for implementation, Urban South did a widespread marketing campaign to publicize their availability. Through the web-based interface, students can now create, save, and update several educational plans. When they choose a degree, the interface provides them with the foundation, intermediate, and advanced courses they will need to complete the degree. With this information, students can then project a course plan over time. Furthermore, students can enter their courseloads and the times they are available for classes and the software will map out when specific courses are available and how long it will take to complete the degree. If a student decides to complete the degree sooner, the software can revise the timeline based on prerequisites already completed, increased courseloads, and changes in the student's schedule. The student can then save the new plan. These educational plans can be kept private or put in a folder for viewing by an advisor or faculty member. A faculty member can click on a name on the online course roster to find out more about a student's educational goals.

Because the state in this instance has developed a standardized course numbering system, a standardized prerequisite system for general education courses, and a standardized format for transcripts, any student who might be interested in transferring to another college can go to a state web interface and perform a statewide degree program search and degree audit. As a result, a student can search by institution type (two-year or four-year, public or private) and by certificate or degree type. The information is provided not only through a link to the college's catalogue, but also through information uploaded from each institution through consistent, agreed-upon formats. The software can pull up the student's unofficial transcript, automatically input the courses completed, and provide the student with information about courses still necessary to finish a degree.

Kalsbeek has noted that information management can be a "boundary-spanning activity that builds bridges between student services and academic areas" (1989, p. 509). In this case, the implementation of online counseling services appears to be having that effect. A vice president at Urban South notes that one of the ongoing challenges is to "sustain change" – to continue to raise expectations. Not surprisingly, this process is not without friction. There are now several cross-functional teams at the college focusing on learning-centered issues and seeking to establish measures that can serve as benchmarks for assessing student outcomes. One faculty team at Urban South has been developing ways to include student self-assessments and career goals in class syllabi and assignments, and this has raised some heated discussions among faculty members not involved in the process. Some of the team's recommendations have been criticized as growing from a process described as "not inclusive," although those making the criticisms had in fact declined to participate.

These kinds of tensions can be – and perhaps should be – considered part of a process that is working well in that these differences of opinion are prompting people to communicate about their vision of the direction of the college and the role of developmental counseling in the classroom. As some indication of the overall success at Urban South, according to a recent survey, 73 percent of students said that they had tied their career goals in to a classroom assignment.

Given the limited resources at many community colleges and the difficulty of working across departments, it may seem almost impossible to develop the sort of campus culture that fosters the creation of the kinds of online tools mentioned. For example, in one case, a dean of student development at Northwest Metro who is interested in improving retention rates has for years been requesting to block the registration of students who are in academic peril until they speak with a counselor. While full-time-equivalent enrollment is increasing at the college, retention has been on the decline. However, the head of student services has not been responsive to the dean's idea, saying that the department has neither the time nor the money to make the change. The dean is continuing to raise the issue at the executive dean's level, trying to get student success to become a more prominent element on the overall college agenda. At this stage, she is building capacity the best way she can: one step at a time.

As previously noted, Suburban West does not have a particularly strong record of effective use of information. It recently received a grant to help create an information culture on campus by developing a better understanding of the extent to which various student interventions affect student success. The college is currently developing a web-based system that will broaden the concept of the online educational plan to include updates related not only to courses taken, but also to tutorial and other student support services received.

As part of this new system, if a professor or an academic counselor recommended that a student attend a math lab or a writing tutorial, the college would be able to track whether the student did in fact receive those services. Through the new technology, the student would attend the lab or the tutorial using a student identification card embedded with a smart chip that would record the visit. Once collected, this data would be fed back to the counselor or the professor. In this way, campus decision makers will be better equipped to track any correlation between certain interventions and student success. Although the project is still in its initial stages, it has generated interest among staff and faculty and is serving as a catalyst for the better use of information campuswide.

Formalizing a Culture of Collaboration

Successful implementation of the kinds of information technologies discussed in this chapter most often requires administrators and staff who traditionally provide student services to work alongside IT staff and faculty in the development of systems that engage students and encourage them to take responsibility for their own learning. In fact, these types of initiatives require not only the cooperation and the collaboration of IT staff and academic and student services personnel, but also a meta-level understanding of the project as a whole. In this way, all stakeholders are clear about their individual and collective functions while a new system is being developed as well as once it is implemented. And while there does not appear to be a single right solution to the implementation of any information system, colleges that can learn from the problems encountered at each stage – planning, design, and implementation –

are often at the forefront of applying new information technologies in response to the various challenges their campuses face. As a result, colleges are better able to support the means for students to become more engaged in their own educational success.

References

Astin, A. (1982). *Minorities in American Higher Education: Recent Trends, Current Prospects, and Recommendations*. San Francisco: Jossey-Bass.

―――. (1984). "Student Involvement: A Developmental Theory of Higher Education." *Journal of College Student Personnel, 25*(4), 297-308.

Ender, K., Chand, S., & Thornton, J. (1996). "Student Affairs in the Community College: Promoting Student Success and Learning." In K. Ender, S. Chand, & J. Thornton (Eds.), *Contributing to Learning: The Role of Student Affairs*. New Directions for Student Services, *75*, 45-53. San Francisco: Jossey-Bass.

Frost, S. (1991). *Academic Advising for Student Success: A System of Shared Responsibility*. ASHE-ERIC Higher Education Report No. 3. Washington, DC: Association for the Study of Higher Education, ERIC Clearinghouse for Higher Education, and George Washington University.

Kalsbeek, D. (1989). "Managing Data and Information Resources." In U. Delworth & G. Hanson (Eds.), *Student Services: A Handbook for the Profession*, Second Edition (493-512). San Francisco: Jossey-Bass.

Pisani, A., & Stott, N. (1998). "An Investigation of Part-Time Faculty Commitment to Developmental Advising." *Research in Higher Education, 39*(2), 121-142.

Chapter 4

Supporting a Culture of Inquiry Through Institutional Research

Two decades ago, different administrative departments with wholly separate computer systems had difficulty sharing even routine information in a timely way. Today, the widespread use of relational databases has made the sharing of routine information much more automated. In addition, use of web-based interfaces can now provide students with access to their own personalized web pages that bring up financial aid statements, prompt them about registration deadlines, let them enroll in a class, or allow them to find out what they need to fulfill their major – all online instead of waiting in line. The same technology can provide a way for administrators to check enrollment levels, for deans to find out which sections are full, and for faculty to learn of any special needs of incoming students. This shift in the way that information can be accessed and applied for decision making has been shaped and shepherded by advances in information technology.

Beyond implementation of these information systems, however, it is essential to keep in mind the importance of building a *culture of inquiry* – that is, a culture that purposefully reflects on its own practices and then proactively creates and implements actions that respond to organizational problems or issues. This cannot be achieved without developing alliances across hierarchies, across disciplines, and among individuals so that people are less likely to be concerned about changes in the way that information is handled or distributed on campus. Even as more community colleges are finding ways to cultivate a culture of inquiry, old patterns may still stand in the way. Although many programs and departments seek better information about their institution and their students, some would rather not know as much about the results, particularly if others are doing the asking. For example, some administrators may be concerned that results will be taken out of context or will be used punitively with good programs that have nonquantifiable results. Others simply fear changes to the way they operate and are wary of losing the methods they have used to get results in the past, even if those results were imprecise or inadequate. For an institution to effectively use information for decision making, these paradigms of concern about data and its use must be replaced by a culture of inquiry.

Within this context, offices of institutional research (IR) at community colleges are charged with overseeing the gathering of data, transforming it into useful information, communicating that information to decision makers, and assisting them in applying it effectively in strategic planning and policy formulation – all with the aim of enhancing services to students and, specifically, improving student learning. This multifaceted role is often a political one as well. While not every community college has the resources to implement data warehouse systems, each community college, regardless of the type of information system it has in place, can take steps toward creating a culture of inquiry among staff and faculty. IR offices can play an important role in this transition.

The Many Faces of Institutional Research

The function and structure of IR in community colleges have undergone significant change over time. The literature on IR attests to the many functions that the institutional researcher has fulfilled, from custodian of data to impartial scholar, and from spin doctor to knowledge manager (McLaughlin et al., 1998; Volkwein, 1999; Serban, 2002).

Transformations in the field of IR can be traced to both internal and external demands. Internally, this includes board members and trustees who want to know how their colleges are meeting the needs of students as well as faculty and staff who must make decisions about the programs and services they offer. External demands have also played a role in shaping IR responsibilities. State reporting requirements, accreditation, and performance-based funding have all contributed to the community college's desire for data and information. These factors put pressure on IR to continuously improve its reporting function as well as to assist the college by providing analysis and contextual understanding of complex research issues affecting a wide variety of community college constituencies.

In many cases, the IR function has become integral to the decision-making process in community colleges. Recognizing the varied roles that IR offices fulfill is important for understanding the sharing and use of information on campuses. McLaughlin, Howard, Balkan, and Blythe (1998) suggest that the role of institutional researcher encompasses three primary functions: (1) as custodians of data, overseeing large databases; (2) as brokers of the process that transforms data into useful information through the writing of reports; and (3) as managers in applying that information to specific situations, such as explaining the impacts of research findings to principal decision makers.

Volkwein (1999) describes IR in terms of four fundamental roles: (1) information authority (educating the campus community about itself); (2) policy analyst (consulting to top management); (3) spin doctor (advocating for the campus to external communities); and (4) impartial scholar and researcher (producing evidence about institutional effectiveness). Volkwein suggests that these are not discrete roles, and that most often IR staff perform these roles simultaneously. Serban (2002) adds a fifth component that augments Volkwein's four facets: institutional researcher as knowledge manager. Serban suggests that IR has the potential to become a catalyst for and is integral to the creation, capturing, and sharing of knowledge.

In short, the institutional researcher can be seen as shouldering at least three distinct, though often intertwined, roles. As *data custodian,* IR offices often work to maintain the data integrity of large databases. This might include making sure that data is properly entered and that common definitions are used in the process. IR offices are sometimes responsible for overseeing the development of data warehouse systems, with broader ranges and new kinds of information accessible in real time to deans and administrators through web portals. Additionally, IR offices might provide tools for others to extract their own data from campuswide information systems.

In the role of *information broker,* one of the primary responsibilities of the institutional researcher is the reporting function, which includes the compiling of data and its transformation into useful information. Methods used range from traditional pen-and-paper surveys to sophisticated data-mining tools. This information is often organized into routine reports, generated weekly, monthly, or quarterly, that offer tabulations of current figures or long-term trends concerning enrollment levels by section, vacant dorm rooms, or classroom use patterns, among other topics. IR offices might identify and analyze significant trends that affect important processes and outcomes, present a limited number of findings, and display compelling and pertinent graphics to illustrate central points. These reports are then distributed to the appropriate decision makers and to staff members who use them to support their own decision-making needs.

At the other end of the spectrum of institutional researcher as *knowledge manager* is the creation of more policy-driven reports required by external accrediting, governmental, or systemwide agencies. Effective dissemination and use of these reports demonstrate the need for astute awareness not only of the technical and substantive issues involved, but also of the political and cultural context specific to the campus. In this role, the IR staff are valued as part of the monitoring and decision-making processes.

The Impact of Technology on Institutional Research

As with most functions within the community college, one cannot overlook the impact that technology has had in reinventing the role and capabilities of the

IR office. For instance, the reporting function is being transformed by technologies that allow institutional researchers to target their audiences and market their materials more effectively. Email reminders allow researchers to reach potential readers – typically staff members or faculty – on their desktops, where users can pull up a report or a specific section of a report applicable to that person's job.

As a further step, the IR office can offer faculty and staff the power to select reporting parameters for themselves through the web. Users can visit a web page where they can choose among pull-down menus that offer several common options, such as viewing enrollment levels by section or by department, comparing enrollment levels to this time last semester or to this time last year, or seeing five-year enrollment trends by specific student subpopulations. Explanations of findings can also be provided with the click of a mouse. Colleges are finding that distributing reports via the web is not only less expensive than printing and mailing the reports, but is also more effective and user friendly.

Likewise, many IR offices are upgrading to relational database systems that allow departments to easily share information. These new systems also enable an IR office to run reports much more quickly, which expedites the delivery of information for use in decision making. And, these systems also provide more powerful ways to sift through data and derive meaningful information.

As a result of these technological changes, the information maintained by IR offices is now much more accessible to administrators, faculty, and staff. Furthermore, web portal capability has brought routine information to the fingertips of decision makers on campus. In fact, many types of ad hoc requests are now routinely available via web access. This has expanded the amount of time and resources that an IR office has available for higher-level information brokering and knowledge management.

This infusion of technology to the function of IR has in some instances put a strain on the relationship between IR offices and offices of information technology. At the very least, it has been the cause for some confusion about the various roles of each office. At many community colleges, a clear division of duties does exist between the IR and IT offices, and this helps stimulate good relations between them. At such institutions, the IR office is typically responsible for all reporting and all decision support, which relieves the IT specialists from those duties. This means that IT can focus on programming, installing, and updating software and hardware, providing software and hardware support for faculty and staff, and generally making sure information systems are functioning smoothly.

Effectively maintaining this division of duties requires more time devoted to communication between offices. At City Southwest, the IR and IT offices operated as separate empires a decade ago, each doing its own thing, with little communication between offices. As a result, IT staff were being called upon to contribute decision-making support, and the IR office was hiring staff with technical and programming expertise. As the college began developing a data warehouse system, IR and IT staff were brought together with other chief stakeholders to plan the system. During these meetings, the IR and IT offices began to transform their relationship. Rather than continuing to operate in separate silos, each began focusing on the areas they handled best and communicating that clearly to each other and to other principal groups on campus, including resource and budget managers. IR began to trust IT to provide technical support in a timely way, and IR helped IT by working directly with faculty on ad hoc reporting requests.

Efforts by IR offices to build bridges must reach well beyond IT offices to administrators and faculty as well. No single road to success exists for partnering with these varied constituencies, and much depends on the information culture and politics at each institution as well as the on place the IR office holds at the decision-making table.

Institutional Research in the Organizational Hierarchy

Working within a multifaceted role, IR offices are charged with satisfying a range of functional goals within the institution. Yet the positioning of IR within the institutional hierarchy is quite varied from college to college. As with any office within an organizational hierarchy, the level of managerial and budgetary support is in part determined by where the office reports. In the case of the IR office, this is likely to determine which substantive issues are addressed and whether the IR function is seen as one of data custodian, information broker, or knowledge manager.

At Suburban Southwest, a midsize community college, the head of IR is on the same organizational level as the deans. Like them, he formally reports to the vice president for educational support and planning. In actual practice, however, the IR director reports to the vice presidents and the president. He not only regularly attends planning sessions with the president and vice presidents, but his opinions are also regularly sought in those meetings. One of his primary functions at these planning meetings is to be a resource about student needs and the college's level of effectiveness in serving them.

At Urban Southwest, the IR director reports directly to the dean of planning. The IR director is capable technically and analytically and has the organizational experience and competence to handle political issues on campus. The dean of planning actively involves the IR director in strategic planning meetings, and the president considers him an integral participant in decision making. In short, the IR function is highly regarded on campus.

Alternatively, at Valley Rural, the head of IR is experienced with technology and can report on substantive concerns but is less experienced in dealing with the broader organizational and political matters that arise in the community college setting. The IR function is housed under the dean of instruction, who has assumed the role of IR in planning sessions with the president and other senior staff. Because of where the IR function is housed, it is very rigorous on issues of student learning. However, other routine and ad hoc research requests tend to be handled by the IT department.

At Southeastern Metro, the IR director reports to the vice provost for education policy and analysis. At first, the IR director was worried when the office was placed under education policy and analysis because she feared that it would become mired in whatever educational movements were popular at the time. However, this arrangement has been effective for a number of reasons. The vice provost values the sharing of information, and thus gives the IR office latitude in fulfilling its duties. Additionally, the office of education policy and analysis is broad enough to emphasize research about student success without dismissing other inquiries about institutional effectiveness.

Southeastern Metro's IR director also enjoys a collegial relationship with upper managers, who are eager for information. While she has a wealth of experience in technical and analytical issues, she also understands the political contexts of information sharing on campus and has been careful to establish the credibility of the IR office as an internal consultant that does not have a vested interest in particular issues or points of view. The office maintains a sharp, analytical focus on the issues that faculty and administrators bring to the table and works to build trust among internal constituents. For instance, if a researcher and a faculty member do not get along, the office assigns a different researcher to the project.

Considering the spectrum of duties institutional researchers perform, it is not surprising that IR directors today need to be politically as well as technically astute in the ways in which they use and share data and information. On the one hand, they develop and maintain close ties to the president and other upper-level managers, who in turn provide them with funding and need them for decision-making support. At the same time, they work closely with deans and mid-level managers, who typically compete with them for funding, yet who also rely on them for timely information about budget levels, enrollment management, classroom use, and student success rates.

Establishing a Foundation of Credibility and Trust

In all these varied roles and relationships, juggling both technical and political responsibilities, institutional researchers must strive to establish not only their own credibility, but also trust in the information they provide. Individuals who attempt to introduce data-driven decision making may be quickly dismissed if the information does not confirm what others believe is true. Others may attack the accuracy of the data. Still others may attempt to counter the data with firsthand, anecdotal evidence that begins, "In my experience...." And finally, some may listen politely to the findings, nod their heads as a new plan is proposed or even adopted, but eventually stonewall any efforts to create new structures for working in a data-driven environment.

At Suburban Waters, the director of IR possesses both the political skills to assist faculty members, deans, and department heads focused on big-picture issues as well as the technical experience to assess and explain which kinds of decisions could be aided through data-driven inquiries. He works to make sure the campus community sees him as both reports manager and internal consultant on technical as well as political and strategic issues. In the process, he has gained the trust of the president, who now includes him in strategic planning.

At Urban Southwest, the IR office has developed a solid reputation for working to provide accurate, timely information to faculty and staff. Time and again the office has come to be valued for grounding discussions in data rather than opinion and for being willing to question assertions based on assumptions rather than on documented data. The IR office begins each year by providing college faculty and staff essential information about the incoming class, such as its size, ethnic and age distributions, primary language uses, and preparedness for college compared with previous years. The office explains these trends in meetings, training sessions, and presentations for all campus committees. It works with faculty and administrators to establish prime objectives for the year. And it monitors outcomes at several points during the year to check the progress of those objectives.

At Valley Rural, the dean of instruction's oversight of the IR function has helped focus IR activities on student learning. The college does not have a state-of-the-art information system, yet the dean has worked for more than a decade to create and institutionalize a culture of inquiry in decision making. In the late 1980s, when the state required community colleges to improve their methods of assessing students for placement in classes, she formed a faculty task force to address the new state requirements and then used that task force to build support for better internal research about student success in general. When a statewide research and planning group began to offer annual training in student assessment and evaluation, the college sent a core team of faculty and staff to this training year after year. A research planning group culled from faculty and staff was formed to provide guidance for the college. Over the years, as faculty members became more familiar with assessment issues and their impact on student learning, they developed a high level of trust for the dean's work, and the faculty senate supported increased resources for IR on student learning. Recently, both as a culmination of these efforts and as a further step toward more effective assessment of student learning, the faculty senate approved a new faculty position in assessment and evaluation of student learning.

In addition to building trust, a community college's IR office can likewise help tear down old paradigms of closed-door communications by fostering broad dissemination of institutional research findings. For example, at Tri-State South, the IR office works with staff and faculty to generate reports on important topics, whether or not they are of a sensitive nature. In communicating the findings on a particularly sensitive issue, the research office sometimes schedules a staff retreat or other forums to explain the findings and to respond immediately to negative feedback. The office also makes an early draft of the report available to the president and will sometimes revise its final report based on the president's comments.

The director of IR at Suburban Southwest has developed a reputation on campus as the one to go to for accurate information and a quick turnaround. On the political side, he is integrally involved in campuswide decision making. He also actively advocates the use of information in decision making, primarily by working with faculty and administrators to expand their comfort levels in using information. He pursues all ad hoc requests for information and follows through by meeting individually with those who requested the information, to explain the findings and explore the subtleties behind them. He is careful to avoid certain dead-end issues that he has learned through experience expend too much of his time without leading to effective actions that improve services to students. He also visits classes as much as possible and attends faculty meetings whenever invited. For committee assignments, he always selects staff development committees to create staff development opportunities that promote research-based inquiry. In protecting his credibility, he is careful not to align with either the administration or with faculty, but to remain independent.

Finally, the director of IR at Suburban Southwest is wielding his own influence to develop advocates who can help facilitate a culture of inquiry campuswide. Soon after being hired, he worked with one of the vice presidents to assess certain trends over time, taking the time to discuss the findings, adjust the parameters of the study, and develop some new, more useful findings. He persuaded the vice president to explain the results at a planning meeting where goals and a course of action were generated to try to improve the outcomes. He followed up with ongoing information about how the institution was doing in meeting its objectives in this area. During this process, he persuaded the vice president to address a professional conference outside the institution to show how institutional research was used in decision making in this particular instance. In doing so, he created an important advocate for a research-based culture of decision making on campus.

Creating a Culture of Inquiry on Campus

The role of the institutional researcher is not only to interpret data, but also to educate others about the value of the information and the potential for using that information in decision-making processes. Providing accurate, timely information is important, but not sufficient. The information must be connected to real issues in real ways. For the IR function, this does not mean simply doing surveys, providing training, and giving presentations. Rather, it requires being at the table in strategic planning meetings and getting others at those meetings to ask for better information surrounding an area of dispute. It requires following up with faculty members who have asked for information, probing with them the contours of the results, and helping them consider actions that can improve those results. Ideally, institutional researchers facilitate a culture of inquiry by becoming experts in understanding and engaging the internal organizational processes and information culture of their colleges as well as getting end users of the information to become active participants. None of this happens overnight.

For example, Urban West, a large community college, developed the capability for faculty and staff to generate reports through the web, but it did not benefit from a long history of promoting information-based decisions on campus. Despite several orientation sessions, use of the system was not widespread. Several faculty voiced fears about the new information system, saying the system reflected a new way for the administration to gain power and discipline departments. As one faculty member summarized the suspicion: Behind every piece of data is a hidden agenda.

By contrast is Southeastern Metro, which over time has developed a strong reputation on campus for effective information management. Its purchase and use of interactive web-based technology fit within an institutional context in which upper management values information and requires informed support from deans and directors who present budgetary and other requests. Since administrators, faculty, and staff can generate their own reports quickly and relatively easily using a web-based interface, fewer ad hoc requests are funneled through the IR office, thereby promoting and reflecting a more decentralized use of information in decision making. A primary reason that the implementation of a web-based intranet has been largely successful at Southeastern Metro is that an information-based culture was already in place.

Successful promotion of the use of information in campus decision making often hinges on at least two fundamental practices. First, building allies among the users of information – those who stand to gain by the implementation of knowledge-based decision making – can help create a culture of inquiry on campus. A second way is to facilitate access to accurate, timely information.

In one example, Suburban Coast has implemented a new data warehouse system that will eventually be accessible to all administrators, faculty, and staff through a web portal. The data warehouse was already in place when the new head of IR came on board. But the system was difficult to access without technical expertise and was infrequently used by decision makers. In fact, hardly anyone outside of the IT office was using it. The IT office was so overburdened with getting the system running that it had stopped taking ad hoc requests for reports. The new IR director had the technical background to work with IT, and she began handling the ad hoc requests herself and prioritizing implementation of the web portal system.

In essence, Suburban Coast's web portal provides users with a web page that can be personalized with various options for routine tasks – in this case, the generation of reports based on pull-down menus the user selects. In implementing the system, the IR director was careful to focus the portal on the kinds of information that each group needed, with pull-down menus that would offer a useful range of report parameters, though not so many choices that users would be confused or overwhelmed. She was also careful not to bring any group online until something was available to them that would help them perform their jobs effectively so that users would immediately perceive the value of the portal. As long as the primary functions were available, other capabilities could be added as the need arose.

She first targeted upper managers by giving them direct access for the first time to budget information and enrollment patterns campuswide. From their own desktops, managers could pull up any department's budget and find out its allocation and spending levels by line item and unit. This increased access to campus data meant that managers could compare such things as travel costs by department and could attend their next budget meeting prepared to argue for parity with other departments. In turn, this meant that the president and vice presidents had to be ready for this broader discussion, and they handled it by asking each manager to support his or her own funding levels by unit or risk seeing their funding levels cut. To stay abreast of these developments, each manager quickly learned how to access the reporting capabilities of the web portal. Needless to say, discussions took place that previously had been off the table. Access to information spawned more, not less, interaction and debate.

The deans were the next group to get direct access to information from the data warehouse through the web portal. After several trainings and presentations by IR staff, they could log onto the website and generate reports about room use, transfer rates, course success, and student success in moving toward graduation. Rather than waiting until the end of the semester to determine campuswide room-use patterns, they could access that information on the first day or two of classes. Therefore, if they had a shortage of rooms for a particular section, they could find out which rooms assigned to other departments were not being used. This was a gold mine of information, and again, a catalyst for interdepartmental interaction and discussion.

The head of IR at Suburban Coast was pleasantly surprised to find that in her next meetings, the deans were clamoring for improved data entry. For years, she had been trying to interest the deans in improving the accuracy and timeliness of the data that went into the system, but until the deans could generate reports on their own, her pleas had fallen on deaf ears. Now the deans were keenly interested in improving data entry. In fact, they began asking to have faculty department chairs trained on the system as soon as possible so that they, rather than IT or IR, could be in charge of routine internal reporting.

In another example of the kind of inquiries available, the deans found that they could compare faculty members or entire departments on various measures of student success. In fact, one dean became interested in faculty success in moving students from entry-level to mid-level classes en route to their major. The dean got a grant from the chancellor's office to drill down into the data and to work with the IR office to identify instructors who consistently appeared to have lower success rates in gateway courses. The grant also provided funding for these instructors to receive training and resources to improve their rates. In this case, access to the information was not used in a punitive way. On the contrary, it brought about increased discussion and exchange of information to better meet student needs and improve student success.

The implementation of web-based reporting capabilities has been successful at Suburban Coast for at least four reasons. First, it was supported by IT staff, who saw it as making their jobs easier, as well as by IR staff, who had enough technical savvy to avoid overburdening IT. Second, important users were brought into the system only when the system had something relevant to offer them. Third, implementation was accomplished within an information culture that did not provide disincentives to those working to use information to improve results. And fourth, implementation was done in a context in which the college president actively supported the use of information in decision making.

Managing Knowledge in Support of Decision Making

IR offices serve a valuable function on campus. At a basic level, they assist key internal stakeholders in tracking trends on student retention and learning. They also interact with and sometimes must appease important outside constituencies through requirements for evaluation, accountability, and accreditation. Through collaboration, team building, and the sharing of information, their potential as agents of change is enormous, particularly in the realm of their expertise, *i.e.*, helping community colleges do a better job of managing that most precious resource: knowledge. In this way, they help their institutions confront the difficult prospects of change.

Experienced IR directors work to establish and maintain the accuracy of their information over time. They understand that the relevancy of their work depends on their credibility. They work to create allies, to use the technology at their disposal to share information, and to otherwise build internal capacity for a culture of inquiry.

One critical hallmark of a college that is well on the road to effectively using information in decision making is the evidence of authentic dialogue. This may be witnessed in a number of ways: the president asking staff and faculty to support their requests with information rather than anecdotes; deans asking that data files be cleaned up; faculty requesting better student outcome information; administrators involving institutional researchers in strategic planning; and researchers partnering with the IT office, faculty, and administrators to identify challenges and help resolve them. But the crucial ongoing element that ties all of these components together is the monitoring of internal processes to make sure that student needs are actually served. Perhaps not surprisingly, programs and departments that are most successful in serving students tend to be the ones that are most interested in monitoring how well students are reaching their objectives and that are willing to shift course to better serve students.

One question with which college leaders must grapple is this: What can be done to improve services to students, and what mechanisms can be put in place to monitor whether the planned efforts are successful? Where a culture of inquiry exists, institutional leaders are well equipped to respond.

References

McLaughlin, G., et al. (1998). *People, Processes, and Managing Data.* Tallahassee, FL: Association for Institutional Research.

Serban, A. (2002). "Knowledge Management: The 'Fifth Face' of Institutional Research." In A. Serban and J. Luan (Eds.), *Knowledge Management: Building a Competitive Advantage in Higher Education.* New Directions in Institutional Research, *113*, 105-111. San Francisco: Jossey-Bass.

Volkwein, J. (1999). "The Four Faces of Institutional Research." In J. Volkwein (Ed.), *What Is Institutional Research All About: A Critical and Comprehensive Assessment of the Profession.* New Directions for Institutional Research, *104*, 9-19. San Francisco: Jossey-Bass.

Chapter 5

Institutional Leadership and Information Use

How are leaders in community colleges using information and information systems to lay the groundwork for organizational improvement and better decision making at all levels of the institution? Community college leaders vary widely in their approaches to encouraging the use of data and information in decision making. While some college leaders may prefer to make decisions based on the context of their own experiences and the experiences of those they trust, others seek to amass the best and most pertinent information that can help provide a context for their decisions. These leaders believe that the use of information is a fundamental building block in the decision-making process.

There seem to be as many theories of leadership and management styles as there are community college systems in the United States today. Many of these theories have been developed based on organizations in the business world, but there is as well a wealth of research material that focuses on management styles in higher education. Where less research exists is with regard to how senior-level management in the community college uses information and information systems to improve planning and decision making throughout the college.

Trower and Honan (2002) found that, not surprisingly, the demand for data and information among college faculty and staff is higher in institutions where senior management is itself interested in gathering and using data and information than it is in institutions where senior management is only tangentially involved in promoting the use of data in decision making. This chapter discusses ways in which institutional leaders support a culture that values the sharing of data and information.

The Strategic Nature of Technology Implementation

As several researchers have suggested, the lasting value of strategic planning is not the plan itself, but rather the process of communication and debate about contested issues among a variety of stakeholders working toward common goals (Cutright, 1999; Keller, 1983). Given this, what many college leaders have found is that when done effectively, implementing new information processes or technological systems mirrors the open-ended, cross-functional, and often messy deliberative process of strategic planning. And it can be argued that it is primarily this connection that gives technology implementation the potential to serve as a catalyst for organizational change.

One of the challenges of leadership in higher education is the decentralized nature of the enterprise itself. Bass (1990) described higher education institutions as utilitarian organizations that function as organized anarchies, which often have unclear and problematic goals. In the community college, mechanisms for shared governance require upper management to consult with faculty on many basic decisions. These consultative frameworks bring faculty into the decision-making processes but are not necessarily structured to build trust between administrators, staff, and faculty. Although deans and department chairs are driven as much by their commitments to the faculty senate as to their college president, at many institutions there are few incentives for faculty to collaborate across departments or even within their own department. On the administrative side, many departments are run like small fiefdoms, with their own separate information systems, procedures, controls, and culture.

Schuetz (1999) has argued that a truly collegial form of governance can be ideal for community colleges, fostering a sense of empowerment, partnership, and vested interest in successful outcomes. Yet many community colleges experience a governance structure that is primarily bureaucratic in nature and driven more toward the protection of staff and faculty rights, satisfaction, and welfare than toward student learning outcomes (Cohen & Brawer, 1996).

As presidents and other campus leaders attempt to move their community colleges toward improvement, many have used strategic planning initiatives to engage faculty and staff in collective thinking about long-term goals, increase collaboration among units, improve communication between faculty and staff, and coalesce organizational drive and energy around agreed-upon common goals. Shugart (1999) has noted that strategic planning and thinking can help establish major goals and themes for the entire community college and can provide a context of stability and predictability that then enables leaders throughout the college to take measured risks.

Effective strategic planning is both people oriented – involving an array of staff and faculty members – as well as information oriented, using information systems to define and establish needs and measure improvement. One example of such a strategic planning process involved a new president of City East College, who used strategic planning to help a divided organization move toward a unified vision of the future. City East had recently been created from the merger of a previously existing community college and a separate technical college and was experiencing low morale among faculty and staff. There had been intense competition for students from community colleges in the suburbs of this medium-size city, and enrollment had been dropping steadily for several years, which in turn had led to decreased state funding.

The president began the strategic planning process by involving staff and faculty in an environmental scan of the needs of the merged entity, which was still represented physically by two separate campuses. This fact-finding and analysis focused primarily on enrollment issues and perceptions of the college. At the time, City East was implementing a new campuswide information system, which was used to help gather information for the environmental scan. This first phase was also directed toward discussion of and agreement on a collegewide mission, strategic issues, and long-term goals, the most significant of which was to relocate to a single downtown campus.

The second phase of the strategic planning process focused on operational-level goals, objectives, work processes, and outcomes. Administrative departments were required to share information, create objectives, and develop procedures to assess their success in achieving those objectives. This second phase extended the planning process to encompass a broader sweep and to include more campus leaders in strategic thinking and information sharing. This phase also created built-in processes for assessment. The committee leading the strategic process was co-chaired by a faculty member and an administrator and included administrators, deans, department heads, faculty, staff, and students. The process took almost a year and a half to complete – longer than originally planned. However, the result was a process and a plan that generated a tremendous amount of buy-in among those who had the most at stake.

During the process, City East created an information-intensive website that included information and updates at every major stage. Information was posted about educational consultants and vendors as well as facilities designs for the new campus as it was being planned and built. This information-sharing tool also turned out to be a useful marketing tool, as the website was accessed heavily not only by on-campus stakeholders, but also by many off-campus community members and business leaders interested in the college's plans.

During the facility development process, the president reassigned a staff member to work half time on technology issues to improve the implementation of the campuswide information system and to make sure the new facilities included the hard wiring and other features necessary for effective work stations, classroom-based technologies, and other information and communication needs. The staff member's job was to enhance communication among campus groups – information technology (IT) staff, faculty, and administrative staff – about campus technology needs and planning. The dedicated staff member helped primarily by facilitating meetings and following through on information sharing.

Campus leadership effectively used information systems to support the strategic planning process through environmental scanning and the use of the website for marketing. By investing in a half-time staff position to facilitate team building related to technology planning, campus leadership recognized that technology planning is a people-intensive process rather than a series of purely technical issues. Therefore, it required communication among and decision making by on-campus groups not particularly experienced with interacting with each other. This kind of planning process could not have occurred without leadership support from the top or without the leadership support for resources and time that such efforts would entail.

In another example, the president at South Rural College has used strategic planning at the systemwide and campus levels to enhance technological development. As part of a statewide strategic planning process, the president has spearheaded efforts to implement effective technology and information systems in community colleges across the state. For example, the state has provided for high-speed internet access at all colleges, regardless of size. This access program also included forming a statewide consortium to purchase web-based library materials as a group.

South Rural has on its own been involved in regular strategic planning processes for the past decade and has ongoing cross-functional teams and committees. As part of the institution's strategic planning, the president set up a contingency fund for innovative projects. Faculty and staff have used the funding to develop and test creative approaches to management and teaching. For example, funding was provided to faculty to develop fully online courses. After developing and testing those online courses, the faculty determined that students performed better with some face-to-face interaction. As a result, they developed more traditional courses with online components.

The presidents at both of these colleges – the college that uses technology and information systems to support strategic planning and the college that uses strategic planning as a springboard for technological development and innovation – have engaged planning as an ongoing activity rather than as simply a means to the development of a final plan. Both college leaders view the strategic plan as a means for further discussion, cross-unit collaboration, and goal setting, rather than as an end product.

Using Information Technology to Organize for Improvement

Examples from across the country attest to how information technology implementations have brought about changes in work patterns, operations, and self-monitoring processes. For example, faculty leaders have transformed their classroom activities; they have revised how they communicate with other teachers and with students outside of the classroom, and, in some limited circumstances, they are working across the curriculum to assess student learning. Senior-level administrators in academic counseling have used information systems and web portals to help students develop individualized learning objectives, track student progress toward those objectives, identify students who are having difficulty, and connect those students with support services. Some leaders of IR offices are implementing data warehouses and web portals that link previously separate information processes, thereby providing individual faculty and staff with direct access to timely information about budget issues, section-by-section enrollment as it occurs, financial aid, and dorm-room usage, as well as trends and patterns concerning student learning.

When a college works to implement these new kinds of information frameworks, it often turns out that quite a few pieces that had previously been operating independently now must be integrated. For that to happen successfully, each of the groups involved must come to the table and identify the kinds of information they need to perform their jobs. Gaining access to that kind of information generally requires a level of information sharing that can undercut current conceptions of organizational control. It also requires reframing work processes, which can be threatening to many employees. As Chand (1996) has noted, the adoption of new technology is almost always accompanied by an increase in the level of employee anxiety. Particularly in the implementation phase, the expected benefits of new technology appear unsubstantial and artificial; the complexity of new systems is intimidating, and the learning curve is threatening. In academic settings, staff and faculty suspect that using new technologies will radically change their established patterns of work and decrease their control. Yet any successful deployment is dependent on employee acceptance and use of the new systems. For that to happen, the college leadership typically must support the new deployment at critical junctures that recur with relentless regularity.

In the late 1990s, South Metro had a piecemeal information system and began a long-term transformation to using a major enterprise system vendor as well as a group of smaller vendors to create an integrated system that could share information more effectively among units. Through the previous information system, each administrative department had built its own information system, which made it technically difficult to integrate information from other databases. Additionally, the administrative units became de facto owners of their information and were not inclined to share it unless there were compelling reasons to do so. The college itself was composed of several competing campuses that also did not share information. Compounding the situation, the IT department functioned as experts who provided each unit with access to the information it needed and controlled, which gave the IT staff a high level of influence and power. In short, the information infrastructure served to exacerbate an existing organizational culture in which there was intense competition for information resources.

The president started the transformation process by forming a technology planning committee whose membership included associate vice presidents of instruction and technology, deans, faculty, student support staff, and IT staff. In hindsight, the process has been quite successful in transforming the information-sharing culture at the college, but according to several of those involved in the process, it also has been very difficult. It took two years simply to get the committee formed and functioning, another year to move from argumentative allegations to the adoption of a technology plan, and a fourth to begin actual implementation of the plan. Administrative staff did not want to have their purchases and minute budgetary decisions available for widespread scrutiny. As a result, they slowed the process whenever they could. Although it was the instructional vice president who proposed the shift to a relational database-type system, even on the instructional side, the different campuses played a zero-sum game. At many junctures, the IT staff would say, "This can't be done," and would come up with exorbitant cost analyses that no one could easily refute.

Yet, at every crucial step of the process, the president at South Metro stepped in and insisted on the end goal – a workable, relational information system – while leaving it to the committee to decide how to get there. The president made it clear that information sharing was a primary goal of the college, and the college was on a fast track to making that happen. During implementation, as individual units came on board, there was significant apprehension among staff. The business office was in a state of chaos for more than a year as it worked to make the general ledger come together from so many different offices and departments. The process required tremendous amounts of communication between divisions, a kind of communication that had not happened previously. As for the individuals who most strongly opposed giving up control of their own information silos, they have either come to accept the new modus operandi or have left the college. In some ways, the process and implementation required and resulted in an organizational shift from supporting the people who owned the data to serving those who needed it.

Now that the information system is up and running, the culture of South Metro is showing signs of positive change. Faculty, deans, and department heads are now able to access operational information in a timely way. Budgets are online and available for all to see. The IT office has changed its outlook from an expert mentality to a service mentality, from a we-can't-do-it to a how-can-we-help-you outlook. The technology planning committee continues to broach and discuss contentious issues and to press forward. The next step for South Metro is to develop a data warehouse initiative that will further democratize access to data and information on campus.

At another community college, Suburban West, the issue of information ownership was paramount. The college, which is situated within a multicollege district, had been successful in developing a web-based interface within its admissions and records department. The interface was developed by a small cohort of interested academic counselors to help them view, on one web portal, student grades and other records as well as the various interventions that had been recommended for and accessed by each student. While this portal has been quite successful in meeting the objectives set for it by the academic counselors, it has grown too big for admissions and records.

The project's owners would like to see it adopted districtwide, so that it can become a widespread, long-term solution to the district's information needs and so that the information can be monitored and analyzed in an ongoing way. However, it is not clear under whose authority to place the system. The dean of admissions and records wants to place it under the institutional research umbrella at the district level. But the dean also knows that the colleges want control over their information processes. If the district chancellor decides to place it under the institutional research office, a struggle for control might ensue, thereby jeopardizing its usefulness. As a result, the dean is now trying to convince the college presidents to demand that the chancellor place the system under the institutional office, in the hopes that making it a college decision might help the pilot project's chances of survival.

As colleges have moved in the direction of opening up access to data, there exist real concerns on campus about ownership and control of data and information. As these examples reveal, each institution has its own information culture and data-ownership challenges that must be taken into account by institutional leaders as they seek to increase access to data and information to improve decision making. Many leaders have met those challenges by organizing cross-functional planning teams that in many ways mirror the open-ended staff and faculty teams involved in strategic planning initiatives. In some cases, college leaders from the faculty and from individual departments can create more-effective processes for sharing information. In the final analysis, if these processes are to be adopted at a broader level in a way that can transform institutional culture, then upper management must eventually play an active role in supporting such change.

Improving the Access, Use, and Sharing of Data

Community colleges that have begun providing deans, department chairs, administrative directors, faculty, and staff with the information they need to make decisions have found that in most cases the increased access to data serves to increase communication among groups and to facilitate reaching common goals. It is also important to note that this is the case within a leadership context where data is used for program improvement.

For example, City Southwest, a large multicampus community college district, implemented a learner-centered information system project that eventually revamped how the college operated its financial system, payroll system, email system, and student services. The project, which required several different vendors, was originally conceived solely as an IT project headed by the vice chancellor for information technologies. But as work on the project progressed, its range broadened significantly. Cross-functional faculty and staff teams were created to design the system. The vice chancellor of employee development joined the group, as did the vice chancellor for business services and the vice chancellor for educational development.

This increase in information exchange occurred at other levels of the hierarchy as well. At each college, students, faculty, and staff became involved in planning and implementation. Slowly but consistently a major shift ensued as people began to interact across functions rather than within their functional groups only. There was increased awareness that each decision affected the entire system, and there was growing interest in understanding how others were using data and information and how that data was defined, gathered, and compiled. People learned about the vocabularies and perspectives of others, from information specialists to faculty members and from budget specialists to academic counselors. This marked a major shift away from working only with those who shared a common perspective.

In another example, the president of South Rural has very intentionally promoted the campuswide flow of information through several means. This ranges from asking for support data and information each time a staff member comes to him with budget or other requests to engaging college staff and faculty in ongoing strategic planning processes that include progress assessment based on agreed-upon indicators. In addition, faculty and staff can access information about operational and administrative decision-making processes through user-friendly web portals.

To expand information sharing in the decision-making process, the president supported the use of web-based forum discussions or chat groups on each significant administrative problem and proposed solution. For instance, if the nursing program needed more space and planned to expand into a faculty lounge, the program director would post the problem and proposed solution as a forum discussion, invite comments, answer questions, and regularly monitor the discussion. In this way, the director used the forum as he would a discussion in a committee or team meeting. Interestingly, what the college found was that more people participated in and provided feedback through these online discussion groups than would typically attend a face-to-face meeting. Administrators and deans also found that good ideas frequently emerged from this format of information exchange.

Another community college, Urban West, recently created a data warehouse and made it available to every full-time faculty member and most staff members through a web portal. Using pull-down menus, faculty and staff can search for information on their own, pulling data about enrollment trends or retention rates, for instance. Before this system was in place, every time deans or faculty chairs needed information about enrollment, they would have to go to the IT office and request the information. IT staff would then run a report. If a vice chancellor ran the report, that person would have to decide to whom it should and should not be distributed – often a political decision. As the vice chancellor of academic affairs noted, because of the sensitive nature of their findings, most reports were not distributed as widely as they should have been if improving student performance was indeed the main priority. Since under the new system everyone already has access to the data, there no longer are questions about who should see it or attempts to restrict its dissemination.

Early on, people did question the accuracy of the data on the system. However, partly because of the widespread availability of the data, deans and faculty chairs in particular have become much more interested in ensuring its accuracy since they are the ones responsible for the information. As people have become more comfortable with the system and have come to trust the accuracy of the data, they have also grown accustomed to getting budget and enrollment information on a daily or weekly basis rather than at the end of the semester.

At Urban West, this interest and trust in the accuracy of the enrollment and budgetary information has spilled into areas that in the past have generated significant dispute and anxiety. These include retention rates and other measures of student success. Long-term trend information about these issues had always been available through the IT office, but whenever reports came out on such sensitive issues, plenty of people questioned the accuracy of the data, and often the discussions never moved past an opening barrage of questions. Now that individuals are accessing for themselves the data about retention and gaps in student learning, there is not only a greater trust of the results, but also a greater willingness to explore quantitative and qualitative issues that the data raise.

Engaging People in Information Processes

Providing greater access to data is a useful and productive way for administrators to expand traditional decision-making hierarchies. However, on campuses that do not have a tradition of making data-driven decisions, simply collecting and disseminating information can lead to suspicion. On the other hand, effective gathering and use of data can lead to additional requests for data and information to explain the original findings. In many cases, the widespread availability and use of data can lead to unexpected organizational improvements that leaders may not, and perhaps could not, have predicted at the beginning of the implementation process.

Successful community college leadership today requires being able to fashion organizations that are open, to create decision-making processes that actually share responsibility and build trust, and to increase access to data so that campus leaders have the pertinent information they need to support efforts to improve performance. Like the strategic planning process, using cross-functional teams to implement new technologies and information systems can help community college leaders more effectively meet the challenges of using knowledge-based decision making.

The process of transforming work habits around new information processes is generally messy, time consuming, and resource-intensive. But the process can help energize staff and faculty, broaden their perspectives, and prompt them to pursue important collective goals and objectives. More democratic access to data and information may in the short term increase pressure on traditional bureaucratic decision-making structures within higher education. But by engaging more people in the organizational improvement process through internal strategic planning and increased information exchange, community college leaders will be much better positioned to confront the growing external demands for greater accountability.

References

Bass, B. (1990). *Stogdill's Handbook of Leadership: A Survey of Theory and Research*. New York: The Free Press.

Chand, S. (1996). "Implementing and Analyzing Operations in Higher Education." In L. Johnson & S. Lobello (Eds.), *The 21st Century Community College: Technology and the New Learning Paradigm*. New York: IBM and the League of Innovation in the Community College.

Cohen, A., & Brawer, F. (1996). *The American Community College*. San Francisco: Jossey-Bass.

Cutright, M. (1999). *Planning in Higher Education: A Model from Chaos Theory*. Presented at the annual conference of the American Educational Research Association, Montreal, Quebec, Canada.

Keller, G. (1983). *Academic Strategy: The Management Revolution in American Higher Education*. Baltimore: Johns Hopkins University Press.

Schuetz, P. (1999). *Shared Governance in Community Colleges*. Los Angeles: ERIC Clearinghouse for Community Colleges.

Shugart, S. (1999). *A Brief Philosophy of Community College Leadership*. Orlando: Valencia Community College.

Trower, C., & Honan, J. (2002). "How Might Data Be Used?" In R.P. Chait (Ed.), *The Questions of Tenure*. Cambridge, MA: Harvard University Press.

Chapter 6

The Impact of External Demands on the Use of Data for Decision Making

State governments, accreditation agencies, and the general voting public have placed greater demands for accountability on K-16 education. Community colleges, along with K-12 and higher education in general, have responded in various ways to these increased external demands for accountability. For instance, in the 1980s, many states began requiring community colleges to develop better matriculation services for new students. This included mandates for the provision of more robust orientation services, more rigorous course placement testing, and more extensive counseling and academic planning services.

During the early 1990s, when many states were experiencing severe budget crises, many state legislators began to develop and demand outcomes-based accountability measures for higher education generally, including community colleges (Burke & Serban, 1998). In 1997, the State Higher Education Executive Officers found that 37 of 50 states used accountability or performance-based reporting (Nettles, Cole, et al., 1997). Also, state accountability objectives began to shift from enhanced learning processes to demonstrated performance results, a trend that has continued through the establishment of indicators for student learning outcomes and performance-based budgeting. According to Burke (2001), approximately 75 percent of states now use performance-based funding.

Likewise, accrediting agencies have significantly revised their requirements and procedures for accreditation during past decades. In general, accreditation organizations have, like states, been moving in the direction of more significant assessments of student learning outcomes. Rather than mandating specific outcomes that are disconnected from existing institutional practices, however, many accreditation organizations are taking a more holistic approach in promoting within institutions a total systems model to student assessment. This model seeks to prompt institutions to develop their own institutional evidence in line with the college's mission and goals; link it to various budgeting, planning, and curriculum development processes; and make decisions based on the results (WASC, 2002).

How have community colleges responded, given these significant developments and changes in external demands? To what extent have community colleges revised their own internal structures and processes in gathering and handling data and information? And most important, have they improved their processes for decision making as a result? As this chapter reveals, while some community colleges are still resisting efforts to adopt systematic approaches to information gathering and use, other colleges have begun to link external demands for information with internal review processes. A smaller but growing number are regularly using assessment outcomes in systematic ways to inform and improve their decision-making processes.

External Mandates and Internal Responses

There is widespread recognition within community colleges that they need to be accountable to a myriad of external organizations, such as federal agencies, state boards, state commissions, state legislatures, regional accrediting agencies, professional program accreditation agencies, and systemwide offices. There is also a sense that many of these agencies and governing bodies develop and articulate their mandates for community colleges based on their perceived needs of their own constituencies rather than on a proven educational practice. In many cases, external mandates have been developed with little input from the colleges themselves. As other researchers have suggested, mandates that are imposed without input from the colleges are less likely to be implemented effectively than those that solicit input and support from the higher education community (Kozeracki, 1998).

Typically, many external requirements for accountability and performance-based outcomes are not accompanied by sufficient funding to pay for the generation and analysis of the data and information required. Those who have worked for decades within community colleges are likely to have seen a flurry of mandates come and go. Subsequently, many take a long-term view that if they sit tight and pay little attention to the spirit of the law, the current mandates will eventually slip by the wayside.

In the late 1990s, for example, one state established almost 40 indicators that all technical colleges in the state had to track. It also declared that in three years, a significant portion of each college's state funding would depend on the college's performance on these measures. Because this was perceived by many of the colleges as a warning, the pressure for each college to perform well on these measures was intense during the first year. Colleges scrambled to generate the necessary numbers. During the first several years, grant money was available to help colleges that were performing poorly on the measures. The funding subsequently ran out as the state budget situation deteriorated. Now, largely due to the current fiscal crisis in many states, no funding is attached to these indicators.

According to the institutional research office at Southeast Rural, these new mandates required a shift in job priorities in the college's IR office for at least the first year. While certain tasks were given higher priority than they previously held, no significant long-term or structural changes were made during this period. When it became clear later on that there would be no funding attached to the performance measures, the college stopped investing in trying to generate accurate data in line with the performance indicators. From the beginning, Southeast Rural perceived the mandates as an external threat, not as an invitation to promote improvement or change. The college, confident of its own reputation, yet already underfunded in many ways, sought to comply with the mandate with as little disruption as possible to existing decision-making policies and procedures around program improvement and resource allocation.

Ironically, though perhaps not inappropriately, the so-called performance funding appears to have worked in reverse: Colleges that were low performers were eligible to receive additional grant funding, while those that performed better were not eligible. And because the state never implemented the mechanism to base funding on results, the state did not reward those colleges that performed well or that responded well to the state mandates.

Interestingly, during the time these state mandates were established, the use of data and information at Southeast Rural was set up to serve two distinct operations. Requests for internal data were handled by individual departments with information technology support and included what were considered basic operational issues such as enrollment, grades, payroll, and classroom use. The IR office, on the other hand, was dedicated to fulfilling external demands for information, such as state and federal reporting requirements. To generate data, the IR office used the existing data structures, made estimates where actual data were not available, and compiled reports based on the results. Yet, no systemic way existed to use this data provided by the IR office to revise or alter instruction or services provided by the college. Therefore, the state's experiment with performance indicators did not bring about changes in the systematic use of data and information at this institution. In this way, it is clear that Southeast Rural considered external demands for accountability and internal, campus-driven demands for information as distinct.

Further complicating the impact of external demands on the use of data and information in community colleges is that these institutions have historically received different and sometimes conflicting mandates from the state legislature and from the statewide governing body for higher education. For example, the director of research at Suburban Midwest noted that the state legislature had been interested primarily in enrollments, grade point averages, and graduation rates, yet the college felt strongly that these were misleading proxies for learning. Because the college itself has a high transfer rate but a very low student graduation rate, the college feared that the state would publish the low graduation figure without an explanation of student goals and the transfer rate. As for the statewide governing body, because it includes four-year colleges and universities as well as two-year colleges, it is not perceived as a strong advocate for the special needs of community colleges. The statewide governing body has had reporting mandates that have at times been at odds with the state's requirements. As a result, each college has traditionally developed separate collection processes and data measures to satisfy each of these as well as other external sources while trying to ensure that all of the measures are accurate representations of the college.

Recently, however, Suburban Midwest has attempted to create a plan that would fulfill the needs of these external audiences as well as its own internal needs for data and information. Part of the impetus for developing this overall plan derived from a shift several years ago in the requirements of the regional accrediting body, which began emphasizing the quality of the entire educational process, including student learning outcomes, rather than discrete quantitative measures that were not tied to planning, budgeting, and other processes. The accrediting agency, like others across the country during recent years, has been focusing on how colleges collect and use data and information that seek to measure, understand, and improve student learning outcomes. A critical aspect of this new approach involves prompting colleges to become more systematic and intentional about (1) gathering information about issues and trends that are important to the college itself and that build toward its overall mission, and (2) using that information comprehensively to promote improvement rather than simply compiling data and statistics to present a positive image in reports.

This transition toward developing and implementing a more comprehensive model has been difficult for Suburban Midwest, not only because it required changing systems for gathering information, but also because it has meant transforming the way people on campus think about assessment and reporting. It has required bringing groups together to look at the entire data-collection process and the student learning experience and to consider how the college should define and measure what is critical in learning.

The state has also begun shifting its approach in ways that are helping the college align its processes for fulfilling internal and external data requirements. Until recently, the state's performance indicators were not college specific; the same indicators were used to measure performance at every community college in the state, regardless of differences in the characteristics and needs of each college's student body. Now, while the state continues to have several core indicators, it is also negotiating performance contracts with each college. In these contracts, the college can emphasize what it considers important aspects of its student population and which learning processes should be improved based on that population and its needs. While many see this as a positive step forward, because much is at stake in these contracts, many on campus are anxious and mistrustful of how the process will work. Each college's base allocation will be tied to the college's success in meeting the requirements of its own performance contract. If a college meets its performance standards, then it will receive its full allotment under the contract, while underperforming schools may have funding withheld.

Meanwhile, the state governing body has begun developing a statewide database that is both complicating and making possible the statewide analysis of indicators that will be included in the various performance contracts. The governing body is requesting that each college send its raw student data on a spectrum of vital issues to the state. In turn, the state will compile this data and create useful information statewide. One problem at Suburban Midwest is that many staff and faculty members do not trust their own data-entry mechanisms. Therefore, while there is sudden interest in cleaning up data to make sure the college's good results are accurately represented, many doubt this can be done in the given timeframe and within the current budget of the college.

Further, Suburban Midwest knows that institutions define terms in different ways and that these definitions can radically change the results of data inquiries. Statewide discussions are ongoing about using common definitions, but much doubt remains as to whether these issues can be decided and implemented in time, particularly since they have significant human-resource and technological repercussions in terms of revising current data-gathering methodologies and systems. Finally, no matter how accurately the data is gathered and compiled, there is great concern that the data will be used out of context and that the college will be punished financially for incomplete data or for results that do not take into account the particular challenges and needs of the student body.

At the same time, Suburban Midwest recognizes that at the very least, it has the opportunity to shape what the state asks for through the performance contract process and through development of the statewide database. Its pressing current challenge involves both internal and external elements: to determine within the college which processes and learning outcomes provide important areas for study and improvement, and to keep the state and the statewide governing board informed of and responsive to what is most practical, equitable, and promising in terms of learning outcomes. This looming challenge is more significant still in that it will require creating and building support for internal systems – from data entry to faculty committee structures – that will incorporate the use and analysis of learning outcomes in decision making.

Many colleges in other states are going through similar struggles to redefine their internal processes for gathering and analyzing data while also fulfilling state and other requirements for accountability and reporting. One mid-Atlantic state has about a dozen accountability measures for all community colleges, half of which are used in performance funding. All of these measures are broad, including such issues as graduation rates and employer satisfaction. The systemwide community college office, as well as the regional accrediting agency, is concerned that the colleges have not been using the accountability results in their more-detailed internal processes of program review. Meanwhile, the colleges complain that their student data is housed in a statewide database that is controlled by the systemwide office. Colleges have been required to develop and submit action plans for improvement to the state but claim that they do not have access to detailed data that can be disaggregated in ways that are useful for developing these action plans or, for that matter, for fulfilling the reporting requirements of other external bodies, such as the federal government. As a result, many of the colleges have developed data processes internally to track specific student trends and outcomes, processes that are expensive and that duplicate state efforts. Some colleges claim that their own data systems are far superior to the statewide system.

Partly in response to these issues, the systemwide community college office has recently posted all of the community college data on its website. Although colleges still cannot disaggregate the data as they would like to, they can at least verify their numbers and can benchmark against other colleges. In addition, the systemwide office is now working to replace the current statewide information systems, developed primarily as financial systems, with a state data warehouse that is more robust in providing access to detailed student learning outcomes. The plan is that this will also provide the colleges with much greater capabilities to improve student learning, such as through instituting early-warning systems that identify students who need academic assistance.

From the perspective of the systemwide office, the existence of the statewide database, combined with the performance-based funding, has resulted in making much better data available for statewide planning. In the past, the state collected data and provided reports, but many of the reports were dismissed as using faulty data, since there was an underlying incentive for colleges to provide inaccurate data. Now, with performance-based funding, colleges are very careful to submit data that are accurate and clean.

In addition, the systemwide office has been working with the regional accrediting agency to support the agency's efforts to help each college develop a research culture on campus. The accrediting agency will be implementing a new requirement that each college develop a quality improvement plan in which the college must (1) identify the student learning outcomes that it will try to impact, (2) plan a realistic and pertinent research project with a two- to three-year timeframe, (3) consider the kinds of data that are available and the kinds of methodologies used to gather and analyze data, and then (4) use the results in systematic decision-making processes. The systemwide office is seeking to develop the state data warehouse in ways that will support this quality-improvement process.

By comparison, one northwestern state has been using a common statewide data warehouse for community colleges for several decades. As in the previous example, the data are provided directly by the community colleges to the statewide office and then compiled and shared with the colleges. The system allows for queries and normalization of information. Currently, while each college has access to its own data, the data are not shared across the system, although there have been discussions to change this so that colleges can make cross-institutional comparisons.

According to the statewide office, a downside of compiling data statewide is that little innovation exists within the state regarding the creation of new or better ways to use data systems to gather and analyze information. On the other hand, a major benefit of having a statewide data warehouse has been to level the playing field for all colleges: There are no leaders or laggers in data gathering in the state. In addition, the adoption of common statewide definitions has allowed for better statewide planning and cooperative problem solving. For example, for several years many colleges denied that they had a problem retaining students, saying that students have a variety of educational goals and that these goals cannot always be assessed accurately. However, because of the common database where all colleges used the same definitions for gathering data, the system was able to track students who had a stated educational goal and who stayed at least one year. The systemwide office reviewed the percentage of these students who stayed a second year, and the results showed that *all* colleges had problems retaining students. Once presented with this information, the colleges recognized that a problem did exist, and they banded together to use the data to ask for funding from the state legislature. What made the effort sustainable was that the colleges could look locally and statewide to determine that retention was in fact a statewide issue that had local impact.

Linking Accountability Requirements to Internal Processes

For many community colleges, one of the significant effects of external accountability requirements has been a reexamination of the role of IR in this process. In fact, the historical impetus for the creation of an IR function within community colleges was driven by external requirements for data and information, including matriculation planning, the evaluation and assessment of student learning outcomes, and, more recently, accreditation (Sanford, 1995; Volkwein, 1999). According to a representative of one regional accrediting agency, about 90 percent of the community colleges in that region have significantly enhanced their IR offices as a result of external requirements that colleges develop more rigorous and systematic processes for gathering, understanding, and using the results of student outcomes assessments. Colleges are finding that they cannot meet the new standards for systematic review and use of assessment information without a strong IR presence.

Similarly, institutional researchers at many colleges have seen their own work requirements change and their status increase within their colleges as more faculty members and administrators come to them to discuss and brainstorm assessment and evaluation issues. IR personnel have not only become more adept at keeping track of statewide trends, but have also become more judicious in sharing that information with important constituents on campus. Many IR professionals are now being asked to review grant proposals and are called to the table at the beginning of projects rather than as an afterthought to complete an evaluation. In sum, institutional researchers at many community colleges are more commonly being viewed as research consultants rather than as data custodians or information managers.

What many IR professionals have reported in this process is not how often they are called to the table, but how serious the various parties are in linking student outcomes assessment and actual college processes. According to a representative of an accrediting body for community colleges, the majority of colleges required to resubmit self-review reports must do so because they failed to clearly link the review of assessment information to budgeting, allocation, and planning processes at the college. That is, too often the colleges have separate plans for student services, teaching and learning, and technology. Accreditation agencies are requiring evidence that these separate plans are linked to each other in ways that support the overall mission of the institution and that they are connected to the assessment of student learning.

Palomba and Banta (1999) have shown that assessment information is of little use if it is not incorporated effectively into existing college processes. They also suggest that the closer the generation of assessment information is to its possible use – such as in the classroom – the more likely it will be used to improve results. Having a strong leader who supports the building of data systems that can link college processes to performance results is important for laying the tracks in this overall effort of institutional decision making. Yet if the college is ultimately to succeed in improving student learning outcomes, the role of faculty is crucial.

Engaging Faculty as a Means for Change

At one community college, Suburban Southwest, new state accountability and accreditation requirements have begun to change the focus of internal analysis from merely looking at institutional processes to actual assessment of student outcome variables. According to IR personnel on campus, while faculty in general have resisted these efforts, many more faculty members are now participating in and contributing to this process. Several reasons were given for this change. First, the IR office has helped convene several ongoing faculty development efforts, including faculty workshops on classroom assessment practices and collecting student data. Second, the IR office sponsors faculty brown-bag lunches that focus on discussing good practices in the classroom and identifying indicators of effectiveness other than grades. And third, the IR office has been active in sending faculty members to outside workshops on evaluation and benchmarking.

College leadership has regularly convened faculty task forces to explore issues related to various student learning outcomes. Even so, it has been difficult to use data to resolve complex political issues. For example, one faculty task force worked with the IR office to complete a comprehensive study of class size in relation to student performance. The study showed that in many classes, and within certain limits, there was no difference in student performance based on class size. Still, many task force members rejected the data, because in the end, the faculty considered the issue to be one of faculty workload rather than student performance.

On the other hand, the IR office at Suburban Southwest also found that faculty members who have participated in the ongoing workshops and explored the findings of evaluation processes for grants have developed new conversations about student populations, the meaning of certain findings, or how to compare indicators to established benchmarks. It is at those stages that the possibilities for change have emerged. As a result, those faculty members and others are becoming more receptive to the full range of questions that outcomes analysis can generate and begin to answer. Interestingly, the IR office has also found that in many cases the faculty members who are most receptive are those whose national professional organizations – such as the Modern Language Association – have begun to discuss and understand the development and assessment of student learning outcomes.

As college leaders and accrediting agencies alike have realized, one way to get more on-campus faculty involved and interested in student outcomes is to link those outcomes to funding and allocation issues. A division dean at Suburban Southwest decided that retention and success would be considered in determining faculty assignments each semester. If a faculty member wanted to receive an overflow class, that instructor's student retention and success rates would have to meet a certain threshold. The faculty union has filed a grievance that has yet to be resolved, claiming that retention and success rates cannot be considered in determining faculty assignments. In any case, faculty in this department have become much more interested in accurate measurements of student retention and success.

During the late 1990s, the IR office at Suburban Southwest received significant levels of new funding that provided an opportunity to distribute funds based on program effectiveness in meeting the college's mission or other priorities. However, all of the new funds were distributed across the board to departments. In many cases, faculty spent funds on pet projects. More recently, as a result of a state budget crisis, the college has been forced to make significant cuts. Now the administration has asked the IR office to assist in the process of determining where to make the cuts, a much more difficult process than determining where to increase spending. But the result has been that program review is now a more rigorous process than in the past, and four programs have been alerted that they may face elimination.

Another community college, Suburban Midwest, has responded to external mandates for developing a systematic approach to assessment by trying to generate on-campus support for participating in a Baldridge-based model. Baldridge, which was developed as a business model to create systematic quality improvement, has been expanded to include many hospitals and K-16 education systems. The approach has helped businesses and nonprofit organizations create a culture that demands and uses data in decision making. Through the Baldridge approach, people at all levels of the organization meet in various groups to discuss and develop performance measures to improve processes and learning and to then track the organization's success in meeting those performance measures. Although the board and the leadership at Suburban Midwest have signed off on the project, there has been faculty resistance. Many faculty are doubtful regarding the appropriateness of this business model for use in a higher education setting, and it remains to be seen whether they will warm to participating in the model.

In comparison with this approach, Urban East has been more forthcoming in generating support among faculty for improving data analysis and student outcomes assessment. Because of some problems the college has had in this area, the faculty senate agreed to create an associate dean position, filled by a faculty member, to handle assessment, accountability, and effectiveness issues related to the college. This position works directly with the IR office, the faculty senate, program administrators, and college leadership to explore issues related to student outcomes assessment and to ensure that the college is ahead in meeting its accountability mandates and in performing well on its accreditation reviews.

In another example, Midwest Metro used momentum built from frustration and from mistrust of the data to bring together a working group of faculty to change the way the college approached student outcomes assessment. As a result of a self-study that was part of an earlier accreditation process, many faculty members became concerned about data-collection inaccuracies, the use of parallel sets of data by different departments, the lack of reliable and consistent ways to share information about effective outcomes assessment, and other issues related to the accreditation review. A faculty and staff working group was formed, a new IR professional was hired to work with the group on these issues, and development of a data warehouse was implemented. The data warehouse project brought in many additional staff and faculty members. While it took several years to develop and create, the data warehouse has improved not only data collection but also the framework for discussions about the use of student outcomes in decision making.

In addition, Midwest Metro has linked program-planning processes to assessment processes. Faculty and staff who want to submit requests for new hires or program expansions must submit action plans that compete with the action plans presented by other faculty members. Each of the action plans must use data and, if possible, assessment information to support the plan's arguments. According to the IR office, the level of questioning among faculty members has grown much more sophisticated. For instance, faculty who propose new programs are now asking questions such as, "How many students do I need to admit to my program if I want to get 20 graduates a year?" This kind of questioning is likely to translate into a cost savings to the college, since program start-ups are based on solid planning rather than hopeful guesses. In addition, faculty are asking questions about comparisons of student continuation rates between departments and in comparison with community colleges with similar student bodies.

Turning Data Into Knowledge

During the past two decades, many states have attempted to increase the accountability of their community colleges through the development and measurement of student learning indicators and by tying results to performance-based budgeting. At the same time, many accreditation agencies are requiring community colleges to develop their own self-review processes that incorporate state-required as well as their own performance indicators and that link assessment results directly to on-campus planning, budgeting, and allocation processes. These student learning indicators and self-review processes appear to be prompting more colleges to use the framework of state-based accountability requirements as an impetus to improve the climate of decision making on campus. On some campuses, this can be seen in the increased importance of institutional researchers charged with helping colleges meet external requirements for information. On other campuses, it can be seen in the creation of faculty and staff bodies and enhanced information-gathering and analysis systems to more effectively respond to both external mandates and internal decision-making needs.

Some community colleges remain apprehensive and distrustful of what these external mandates represent, and so they continue compiling reams of data and submitting reports without integrating the accountability measures into their internal decision-making processes. However, those community colleges are rarer today. As more community colleges – and principal stakeholders within them – become convinced of the need for turning data into something measurable and understandable, more are inclined to take the next step of turning that institutional knowledge into action to improve internal processes and student learning.

References

Burke, J.C., & Serban, A.M. (1998). "State Synopses of Performance Funding Programs." In J. C. Burke & A. M. Serban (Eds.), *Performance Funding for Public Higher Education: Fad Or Trend?* New Directions for Institutional Research *97*, 25-48. San Francisco: Jossey-Bass.

Burke, J. (2001). *Accountability, Reporting, and Performance: Why Haven't They Made More Difference?* Keynote Address, 39th Annual Conference, Research and Planning Group for California Community Colleges.

"Evidence Guide: A Guide to Using Evidence in the Accreditation Process: A Resource to Support Institutions and Evaluation Teams," Working Draft. (2002). Alameda, CA: Western Association of Schools and Colleges

Kozeracki, C. (1998). *Managing Organizational Change in the Community College.* Los Angeles: ERIC Clearinghouse for Community Colleges.

Nettles, M., Cole, J., et al. (1997). *Benchmarking Assessment – Assessment of Teaching and Learning in Higher Education and Public Accountability: State Governing, Coordinating Board and Regional Accreditation Association Practices and Policies.* Stanford, CA: National Center for Postsecondary Improvement.

Palomba, C., & Banta, T. (1999). *Assessment Essentials: Planning, Implementing, and Improving Assessment in Higher Education.* San Francisco: Jossey-Bass.

Sanford, T. (1995). *Preparing for the Information Needs of the Twenty-First Century.* New Directions for Institutional Research. San Francisco: Jossey-Bass.

Volkwein, J. F. (1999). "The Four Faces of Institutional Research." In J. F. Volkwein (Ed.), *What Is Institutional Research All About? A Critical and Comprehensive Assessment of the Profession.* New Directions for Institutional Research, *104*, 9-19. San Francisco: Jossey-Bass.

Chapter 7

Informed Decision Making in the Community College

The information needs of community colleges are growing increasingly complex, while pressures to improve results reach to every function of the college. In community colleges across the country, faculty members, staff, and administrators are working to improve the ways that data and information are used within the college to enhance educational services and student outcomes. As the many examples in the preceding chapters describe, community colleges throughout the United States represent the full spectrum in terms of how they use data and information to support decision making and how they transform knowledge into action.

Some colleges, for example, have instituted new information systems to collect and use student data more effectively but have not been as successful in transforming that data into useful information through dialogue, discussion, or other deliberative processes. Other colleges have extensive processes in place to discuss assessment issues, enrollment trends, or other information among faculty, staff, and administrators but do not have effective data-gathering efforts in place to support their analyses. And in general, of the colleges that do gather data, discuss its meaning, and use the resulting information to make decisions about programmatic changes, few take the next step of evaluating the effectiveness of new programs and initiatives through an iterative process of additional data gathering and study.

As community colleges seek to improve their academic instruction and student services to enhance student learning, it is crucial to first understand the wide-ranging needs for data and information, and second, to look at how turning knowledge into action can foster development of a culture of inquiry on campus. The first involves efforts by community colleges to collect data and transform it into information that can be applied to decision making within a local context. The second involves efforts to use the resulting knowledge to implement programmatic change and take subsequent actions that in turn lead to renewed data collection, analysis, and research. Exploring this *cycle* in which data collection and information analysis supports action that leads to further analysis is the focus of this chapter.

The Wide-Ranging Needs for Data and Information

In many ways, data collection is the building block of the decision-making process. For instructors to know whether particular student interventions are successful, they need access to data about the results of those interventions. Likewise, for deans to know whether to expand the number of sections of a particular course, the college must collect timely data about the numbers of students enrolling in each section and disseminate that information to deans and others. Although technological systems can easily accomplish these kinds of data-collection tasks, implementation of such systems can itself be problematic. As the previous chapters illustrate, a good deal of human knowledge and interaction is necessary to decide, among other things, how to set up the most appropriate technological systems, which kinds of data are important to track, and to whom to make the data available.

Yet many colleges have found that before such decisions can be made, all appropriate stakeholders must be invited to the discussion table. After these initial decisions are made and the new technological systems are implemented, ongoing working groups at the college must grapple with implementation issues that affect faculty and staff. These include training for employees affected by the technology and revision of work processes and job descriptions to accommodate new ways of tracking and retrieving data. Each of these decisions and processes in turn affects the extent to which the data are collected accurately and the extent to which the data prove useful for ultimately enhancing programs and services.

As the previous chapters also illustrate, transforming data into information that is useful for decision making and action is likewise a human-intensive enterprise. Raw data – that is, numbers in a chart or percentages on a spreadsheet – are meaningless without taking the time and effort to interpret the data within a local context. Moreover, significant disagreements exist concerning many of the most important issues facing community colleges. For instance, faculty members might disagree among themselves or with a dean about whether grades, test scores, student portfolios, persistence in the major, or all of these combined are accurate measures of student achievement. Some community colleges have committee structures or other formal or semiformal processes in place for analyzing and understanding assessment; other colleges do not. But in many community colleges, job requirements and expectations formulated during the past few decades have been affected significantly by changing information needs that dramatically affect daily routines. These shifts in job requirements and expectations, as well as the perils of information overload, are very real for faculty, staff, and administrators.

The following summaries of the types of data collection and information analysis efforts taking place on community college campuses are drawn from each of the preceding chapters. These summaries highlight not only the increased data and information needs of community colleges, but also the impact that these internal and external demands for data and information are having on faculty and staff roles and communication.

Academic Instruction. Community college faculty members, whether full- or part-time, face an expanding universe of research on teaching and learning generally, and on their fields specifically. In these tight fiscal conditions, college and university budgets have decreased funding for staff and faculty development and for conference travel. At the same time, the responsibilities of community college faculty are expanding. They are being asked to teach a population that has a wide range of academic preparedness, to understand which teaching and learning strategies are most successful, and to be more involved and informed about complex student assessment issues, from college entrance and placement to student learning outcomes. And they are also being asked to collaborate with local high schools to improve student transitions from high school to college and with four-year colleges and universities to improve transfer rates.

Many faculty members feel overburdened by bureaucratic information processes required for curriculum development, program approval, and student assessment. They often have access only to rudimentary information about trends in student outcomes, particularly by demographic group or other specific criteria. In many cases, they feel removed from the information-gathering efforts and the management decisions of the college, and they have legitimate concerns about the accuracy of data that is available. Finally, many faculty members have experienced situations wherein classroom data have been taken out of context and distributed to external bodies with potentially damaging results for programs and students.

Within this overall context, faculty members at community colleges have taken a variety of approaches to improve data collection and information analysis. In many cases, colleges that have a track record of not using data effectively and fairly are also facing the most difficulties in having faculty use and otherwise participate in new data-collection systems. For instance, when one college instituted a new web-based portal that connected faculty members directly to student data, the administration sponsored an information campaign about the new system and offered faculty training on how to use it. However, because of the historical use of data on campus, faculty had little interest in participating in the new data-retrieval and dissemination efforts.

Conversely, other colleges that had regularly involved faculty members in information collection and dissemination experienced more-effective implementations of new information systems. Strategies used by colleges to build trust for data collection include creating a faculty position in charge of assessment; creating multidisciplinary faculty task forces focusing on such areas as assessment, portfolio review, and technology implementation; promoting faculty attendance at statewide training; and, perhaps most important, regularly asking for data and information from faculty whenever they request programmatic or other enhancements.

In some cases, outside funding through grants and other means has been an important way to begin devoting resources to these kinds of efforts. But at the end of the grant cycle, many colleges have found that to bring lasting changes, internal resources must be devoted to the efforts. In short, many community colleges have found that two elements appear critical to the development of effective data collection and analysis throughout the community college: (1) developing and maintaining a longstanding commitment to the use of data and information in decision making; and (2) connecting faculty members in real, ongoing ways to the processes involved in data collection and analysis.

Supporting Student Learning. Academic counselors and other student services personnel are also burdened by growing demands on their time. As enrollments have begun to swell in many states, many community colleges have not had the resources to increase student services staff proportionately. In several of the colleges, student services personnel reported feeling superfluous when they sought to develop closer, ongoing ties with faculty despite the fact that, for many students, student services have proven integral to their success. Meanwhile, new requirements and external demands are being placed on colleges to show improvement in retention rates, graduation rates, and other measures of student success. Subsequently, colleges are placing additional obligations on student services staff to assist in reaching these goals.

Given the expansive mission of the community college, colleges are finding that developing more effective ways to establish and monitor student educational plans is crucial in assisting students with reaching their academic goals. Many colleges have used technology implementations to help students and counselors establish records of students' educational goals. This is particularly useful in districts where students take courses and access student services at more than one college, so that counselors at any college can easily retrieve student records. The technological implementations have ranged from scanning written educational plans and transcripts to using web-based systems in which students enter and update their educational plans and access transcripts and other information, all of which is available to academic counselors.

Some colleges require that educational goals be established and recorded through the application process. Others require them to be developed in student orientation meetings. And still others require students to meet one on one with a counselor to develop their plans. The most sophisticated systems include automatic mechanisms that monitor student progress toward their goals and trigger information to be sent to counselors at strategic points when progress is not being made or when course taking diverges from a student's original educational plan.

Colleges have developed online counseling services that allow students to communicate in real time with counselors through chat sessions, without having to go to the office and wait in line to meet with a counselor face to face. Also, some colleges have implemented early-alert and other systems that, at significant points in the semester, identify students having difficulty in certain classes and send them a letter requiring them to seek advice from their instructor or to participate in tutoring. In some cases, faculty members and student services personnel have disagreed about the kinds of interventions needed. Colleges that have successfully implemented these systems have done so through ongoing task forces or other mechanisms to bring together faculty members and student services personnel to discuss these issues. One sign that systems such as these are working is that despite, or perhaps because of, the disagreements that have developed, the systems that have been implemented are prompting greater communication between faculty and students and between faculty and student services personnel about the students' work.

Supporting a Culture of Inquiry Through Institutional Research. Perhaps more than any other function at the community college, institutional research has changed noticeably during recent decades. These changes have coincided with advances in technology and increased external and internal drives for campuswide improvement. Twenty years ago, it was not uncommon for different administrative departments within the same community college to have wholly separate computer systems that made it difficult to share even routine information in a timely way. Today, the widespread use of relational databases and web-based interfaces has made the collection and sharing of routine and specialized information much more automated. These new systems enable IR offices to expedite the delivery of information to those who need it for decision-making support and to sift through data and derive more meaningful information from it.

This shift from separate computer systems in each department to relational databases and web-based interfaces is taking place at varying rates in community colleges across the country. Many colleges have lacked the resources to purchase the hardware and software needed to establish campuswide or districtwide databases. Many that have invested in such technology have experienced significant resistance among administrators, faculty, or staff in implementing those databases. In a number of these situations, IR offices have played instrumental roles in seeking to improve the use of such systems.

Meanwhile, IR offices have seen their own duties expand to include at least three principal realms: (1) data custodians, (2) information brokers, and (3) knowledge managers/consultants. As data custodians, IR offices often work to maintain the data integrity of large databases. Among other tasks, this has included helping different campus groups reach agreement about the kinds of data to collect, making sure that data is properly entered, ensuring that common definitions are used, and providing tools for others to extract their own data from campuswide information systems. For information brokers, a primary responsibility is the reporting function, which includes the compiling of data and its transformation into useful information. In their reports, IR offices might identify and analyze significant trends that impact processes and outcomes, present a limited number of findings, and display compelling and pertinent graphics to illustrate central points. Finally, as knowledge managers, IR professionals are finding that they are being called on at the beginning of a project – in its planning stages – as opposed to the end, when an evaluation is needed. At some colleges, IR is brought in to help faculty determine, understand, and improve student retention rates; to help upper management respond to the need to increase or decrease services; or to help academic counselors determine how to improve interactions with students.

In each of these overall realms, IR professionals also serve a very important additional function: to educate those on campus about the opportunities and the real challenges of using data and information to support ongoing learning. Providing others with experiences in using, understanding, and sharing data and information is itself an educational process requiring time and resources. Often, the IR professional must make delicate decisions about whom to include in which kinds of meetings, and at what stage of the process. Considering the range of duties that IR professionals perform, it is not surprising that they need to be both technically and politically astute in the ways in which they use data and information.

Institutional Leadership and Information Use. Community college presidents and senior-level administrators not only face the challenge of trying to manage and guide an organization that is decentralized and bureaucratic in its decision-making processes; they also face external demands for greater accountability and internal demands for shared governance. Some presidents have implemented strategic planning processes to break down information silos and to engage faculty and staff in collective thinking about long-term goals. Others have adopted long-term, open-ended commitments to strategic planning to increase collaboration among units and coalesce organizational drive and energy around common goals.

Several researchers have suggested that it is the process of communication and debate about contested issues among a variety of stakeholders working toward common goals that provides the lasting value of strategic planning – not simply the plan itself. In many ways, implementing new information and technology systems, when done effectively, mirrors the open-ended, cross-functional deliberative processes of strategic planning. For example, when colleges implement new information systems, it often turns out that quite a few processes and databases that had been operating independently must be integrated. For that to happen successfully, each of the groups involved has to identify the kinds of information they need to perform their jobs. Gaining access to that kind of information generally requires a level of information sharing that can undercut previous conceptions of organizational control, which can be threatening to unit heads. It also requires revising work processes, which can be threatening to employees. The benefits, however, feature streamlined information and work processes, greater access to operational information in a timely way, and, most important, greater collaboration in reaching common organizational goals. These features make technology implementation time consuming and disorderly, yet also promising as a tool for bringing about organizational change.

The Impact of External Demands on the Use of Data for Decision Making. There has been a significant increase in external demands for accountability in higher education, and specifically in community colleges. Some of the most significant sources of these external demands have been state governments and accreditation agencies. In general, the accountability objectives of states have begun to shift from enhanced learning processes to demonstrated performance results. This trend has continued through the establishment of indicators for student learning outcomes and performance-based budgeting.

Accreditation agencies have been moving in the direction of more significant assessments of student learning outcomes. Rather than mandating specific outcomes, however, many agencies are taking a more holistic approach in promoting within institutions a total-systems model of student assessment. The goal of this model is to enable a college to develop its own means of evaluating student and institutional effectiveness in line with its mission and goals, and to make better-informed decisions based on the results.

Community colleges have responded to these external demands through a variety of processes for data gathering, information analysis, and reporting. In many cases, colleges seek to follow the letter rather than the spirit of the new requirements. They scramble to generate the necessary numbers for the state and to compile a paper record of planning and budget processes that appear to be tied to assessment issues. In many cases, state requirements and budgeting shift so dramatically over the course of a decade that there are long-term fiscal benefits to the wait-and-see approach.

Many colleges are moving to develop, in compliance with the new approach of accreditation agencies, more comprehensive internal data and information processes that fulfill their state's requirements for meeting performance criteria as well as their own internal needs for better understanding of student learning outcomes. Rather than simply compiling data and statistics and trying to make it all look impressive in reports, colleges are required to determine the kinds of issues and trends that are important to the colleges themselves in reaching their mission, and then using that information in planning, budgeting, and other regular processes to promote improvement. This in turn requires building support on campus among staff, faculty, and administrators for internal systems – from data entry to faculty committee structures – that will incorporate the use and analysis of learning outcomes in decision making.

As these summaries of the data and information needs of community colleges suggest, many of the challenges that arise in using information more effectively derive from organizational rather than purely technological procedures and constraints. In each of these areas – from academic instruction to external demands for accountability – having effective technological systems in place is a necessary, though on its own not a sufficient, condition for supporting faculty, staff, and administrators as they seek to make informed decisions.

Turning Data Into Knowledge and Knowledge Into Action

The preceding summaries and chapters describe some of the challenges and accomplishments of community colleges that are seeking to use data and information more effectively to improve services and student outcomes. Based on the extensive interviews completed for this book, it is clear that institutions have developed distinctly individual processes for dealing with their expanding needs for improved data and information on their campuses, and that no one approach will work for all colleges. Even within a single community college, a process or system that proves effective for one academic or administrative unit may have limited success in another.

Data collection and information analysis can be thought of as essential elements that support effective decision making. Similarly, using that data and information to develop a body of knowledge and to implement action can be considered the outgrowth of effective decision making. Turning knowledge into action features the efforts by colleges to share information internally through collaborative and other deliberative bodies, use the resulting knowledge to implement programmatic change, and take other actions that in turn lead to renewed data collection, analysis, and research.

Organizations that employ strategies for collecting, handling, and distributing data are engaged in data or information management, commonly known as data-driven decision making. When these organizations regularly engage a cross-section of principal stakeholders in authentic dialogue and action to improve outcomes, and then also examine the effects of proposed interventions through further data-collection efforts, they take the additional step of developing a comprehensive, information-based culture of research and inquiry on campus. Making data widely accessible to those who need it and sharing information through committee and other deliberative processes are two crucial components of turning data into knowledge and knowledge into action.

Increased Access to Information. With the assistance of new database technologies, many community colleges are moving in the direction of allowing access to data to more people within the organization, with appropriate safeguards for student privacy. This increased access is being sought with the understanding that people at every level of the job hierarchy can perform their jobs more effectively when they have timely access to the data they need. While increasing access to data might be uncomfortable for those who in the past have controlled the release of that data, doing so can, over the long term, help the college focus on its mission and goals.

As many of the examples in previous chapters reveal, increasing access to information is a people-centered as well as a technology-intensive process. Historically, some of the standard venues that community colleges have relied on to release information to the campus community have included annual fact books, periodic research briefs, and newsletters focused on specific issues related to survey results or student outcomes. More recently, college websites with email and listserv notifications of reports and findings are being used more frequently to reach a wider audience. Further along this spectrum is the use of relational databases that provide appropriate people on campus with access to up-to-date information on departmental budgets, student enrollment patterns, dorm and room usage, and student retention and other outcomes data. Many community colleges have taken the leap to developing integrated information systems to replace stand-alone systems that had been built separately by each department or each campus and that previously served to encourage a culture of information hoarding rather than a culture based on sharing data and information.

These shifts toward greater access have not taken place without difficulties.

For example, some colleges begin implementation of a major information system with the assumption that it will remain an information technology project. They staff an IT-led committee, only to find that the project quickly expands beyond the planned scope as IT specialists realize that they do not have the expertise to determine how the information will be treated. The more successful community colleges have brought together an array of people to ensure that technology plans are successfully implemented.

Once implementation of an information system is under way, there are additional challenges associated with getting people to use it. Some colleges invest in extensive marketing efforts, while others invest more heavily in professional development for employees. In many cases, however, having a committee of administrators, faculty, and staff who have worked on the implementation from the start adds an important element to the success of the implementation. Many colleges have found it important to phase in new technologies – for instance, getting a core group of counselors to pilot a new online counseling service, or giving faculty course relief to be trained in using a new system, then in turn training others in their departments.

While increasing access to information has presented community colleges with some unexpected challenges, it also has produced unanticipated benefits. For example, colleges have found that giving managers direct access to budget information and enrollment patterns campuswide has allowed them to pull up department budgets and determine allocation and spending levels by line item and unit. Access to this information meant that for the first time, managers could compare expenditures such as travel costs by department and could then attend their next budget meeting prepared to argue for parity with other departments. In instances such as this, increased access to information may actually result in many more interactions and debates taking place than had previously occurred. But even where disagreements about interpretation emerge, these conversations can serve as a catalyst for discussions that lead to further improvements in internal processes.

Increased access to data for a wider audience than in the past also has the effect of providing end users, rather than IR professionals or upper management, with the tools to make informed decisions. This allows users to make stronger cases for implementing a new program or revising a service. For example, many colleges are seeking to increase faculty access to and involvement in the analysis of student enrollment, retention, and assessment data. In some colleges, faculty are meeting within their departments to try to improve student outcomes. In other colleges, faculty have set up cross-departmental teams to study student learning outcomes. Still other colleges have created new faculty positions charged with improving the colleges' understanding of assessment issues. Regardless of approach, sharing data and analyzing information in cross-departmental teams can help build a research-based culture and bring about new efforts that participants could not have envisioned at the start of the process.

There are also many examples of community colleges increasing access to data for student users to help them take a more active role in their own educational and career planning throughout their college experience. In many cases, this features making information and processes for enrollment, registration, housing, and even academic counseling available to students online. In addition, degree-audit systems, early-alert systems, academic-related interventions, and developmental advising are all ways in which colleges have used information systems to engage students continuously in their own educational planning and success. Other colleges have developed web-based portals or information systems that enable students to perform certain functions online, such as viewing their grades, completing surveys on life and career goals, finding out about degree requirements, and creating and updating their own educational plans.

At a minimum, these types of implementations require that administrators and staff who traditionally provide student services work side by side with faculty to develop systems that encourage and engage students to take greater responsibility for their own learning. If the implementations involve transfer or course articulation with other community colleges and between two- and four-year institutions, then the information sharing necessarily involves staff and faculty at more than one institution, an even more fundamental challenge.

The Feedback Loop. As colleges work to increase access to data – whether for administrators, faculty, staff, or students – they are finding that this increased access requires sharing information through formal or informal deliberative processes. That is, what all of the previous examples have in common is the involvement of teams in processes that connect and engage. In many cases, the teams are cross-departmental; include administrators, faculty, and staff; and bring together upper as well as mid-level management and staff.

Once incentives and work habits begin to form around information sharing within the institution, the greater access to data and increased flow of information throughout the organization can be used to establish a feedback loop, a process to continuously monitor the results of actions taken. For example, if a new program is launched, a feedback loop is used to find out what enrollment levels the program attains during the first semester, or during the second semester. Similarly, if a program is enhanced, what effect does that enhancement have on student retention or student persistence toward a major? And if a new service is implemented, which groups of students are using it, and to what effect?

For example, one college applied for and received a federal grant that required the tracking of student progress and the monitoring of outcomes. The college then used the information to create interventions outside the classroom. Even when grant funding ceased, use of the student-tracking database continued with support from the faculty. As faculty members have gathered information, placed it within appropriate contexts, and generated clarifying questions, they have become more comfortable having the college compile data and are more willing to engage in discussions about its use for analysis and improvement. Use of the student-tracking database has also increased collaboration and exchange of information between faculty and academic support staff.

Building Capacity to Improve Student and Institutional Success

It is important to note that each step along the way in fostering a culture of inquiry on campus – data collection, information analysis and management, and turning knowledge into action – is significant in and of itself. The gathering and sharing of data faces its own difficulties and challenges. In many organizations, not everyone trusts the data or accepts the value of using data as the building block for decision making. Many faculty and staff members claim they have direct experience with those who appear to manipulate data for their own purposes or who seem to use information only when it enhances their argument or supports their point of view. Working to effectively collect and share data and to examine the results fairly and accurately is itself an educational process that requires staff development resources and time.

Contextualizing data and thereby creating useful information that contributes to an institution's body of knowledge raises additional challenges and questions. For example, who should receive the information and to whom does it belong – those who asked for it, or those who need it to perform their jobs? What other information is pertinent and should be included? How should the information be presented? How accurate and appropriate is the analysis? How should the information be used, and by whom? No simple answers exist for such questions, and all answers depend on the experiences of the individuals at the table, the nature of their support from above, and other circumstances specific to the college.

Finally, transforming knowledge into action and evaluating the results of those actions presents a whole different set of challenges for community colleges. How accurate are the student outcome measures used? How have programs been implemented and evaluated in the past? Who is charged with making decisions about performance? To what extent should program funding be connected to performance results? What resources are available to explore the data further and to experiment with ways to improve results? Some of the answers to these questions will depend on how decisions have been made at the college in the past. For instance, has information been used to penalize programs, to reward them, or both?

Each community college must cut its own pathway to improving the use of data and information in decision making; using the resulting knowledge to implement actions; and establishing evaluation methods that lead to further data collection, analysis, and research. Some community colleges have endeavored to jumpstart the process by implementing new technology systems. Some have invested in new faculty positions dedicated to improving student assessment. Others have sought grants to bring staff and faculty together to solve persistent gaps in student learning. And still others have participated in rigorous staff and faculty development. Depending on the specific context and the objectives of the college, each of these avenues may prove useful and effective in creating organizational change.

However, no matter which means are used, the most necessary elements for success are (1) bringing people together in truly deliberative processes and with real objectives at stake, (2) supplying them with access to accurate data and information on which to base their decisions, and (3) providing them with the supportive environment they need to evaluate the results and make informed decisions. Only then will the actions that are taken help to build the capacity of community colleges to improve student and institutional success.

About the Author

Lisa A. Petrides is president and founder of the Institute for the Study of Knowledge Management in Education (ISKME), a nonprofit educational research think tank located in Half Moon Bay, California. ISKME conducts research that seeks to help educational institutions advance their capacities to use data and information to improve student and institutional success. The institute conducts research studies about how data and information are being used to transform decision making and align internal and external demands to improve student success. ISKME also conducts organizational impact studies on information technology implementations and evaluations of the overall impact of knowledge management on education programs.

A former professor in the Department of Organization and Leadership at Columbia University Teachers College, Petrides' research and teaching interests are in the areas of information technology, knowledge management, information and decision making, and issues of access and equity in education. She has worked with a wide array of internet-based technologies for classroom teaching. She received a Ph.D. in Education from Stanford University and an MBA from Sonoma State University, and was a postdoctoral fellow in Educational Policy Research Division at Educational Testing Service.

Her publications include "The Squeeze of Accountability in Higher Education: The Challenges of Using External Mandates to Create Internal Change," in *Planning for Higher Education*; "Strategic Planning and Information Use: The Role of Institutional Leadership in the Community College," in *On The Horizon*; "What Schools Have to Teach the Corporate World," in *KM Review*; *Knowledge Management in Education: Defining the Landscape*, a monograph produced by ISKME; "Knowledge Management for School Leaders: An Ecological Framework for Thinking Schools," in *Teachers College Record*; and *Organizational Learning and the Case for Knowledge-Based Systems*, in New Directions for Institutional Research.